Swing Trading
Simplified

By Larry D. Spears

Foreword by
Larry Swing
MrSwing.com

MARKETPLACE BOOKS
Columbia, Maryland

MARKETPLACE BOOKS

Simplified Series

Technical Analysis Simplified
by Clif Droke

Elliott Wave Simplified
by Clif Droke

Moving Averages Simplified
by Clif Droke

Gann Simplified
by Clif Droke

Support & Resistance Simplified
by Michael C. Thomsett

"The driving principle of the swing concept is that you deal only in stocks that are already moving in an established trend — and you open only those positions, either long or short, that will profit from a continuation of that primary trend. Thus, whether experienced pro or swing novice, you have strong market forces on your side in every trade you do."

—Larry D. Spears

This and other Marketplace Books are available at discounts that make it realistic to provide them as gifts to your customers, clients and staff. For more information on these long-lasting, cost-effective premiums, please call John Boyer at 800-272-2855 or e-mail him at john@traderslibrary.com.

ISBN 1-59280-063-7

Printed in the United States of America

Contents

Appendices:

Resource Guide

About the Author   119

Foreword

Traders and investors study markets through price charts. These powerful visual tools offer a common language for all stocks, options and indices. The theory behind this is called "technical analysis." Technical analysis begins with a simple observation that all market action is reflected in the activity of price and volume over time. This information creates a profound visual representation when properly presented in a chart. Prices rise and fall, with rising prices being stimulated by greed and falling prices by the awakening of fear. This emotional tug of war between greed and fear generates a "swinging" price movement that provides the perfect opportunity for "Swing Trading."

Swing traders capitalize on the emotions of others while they carefully control their own emotions and systematically enter and exit trades. Swing traders recognize the levels of support and resistance. They understand the concepts of momentum and volatility, and can identify a trading range or channel.

Equity trading provides a natural arena for swing traders. As price seeks an equilibrium state, swing traders seek to exploit direct price thrusts as they enter positions at levels of support and resistance. By examining chart pattern characteristics, they make money in both trending and range-bound markets. Swing trading is a classic strategy that involves holding stocks for a short period of time — typically from a few days to a few weeks. Unlike day trading, swing trading is independent of time — though some swing traders will prefer to exit a slow-moving position and move on to a new opportunity.

Swing trading is very popular among short- and medium-term traders. It offers many virtues compared to the hyperactivity of day trading. With recent changes in SEC regulations that affect the way brokerage firms administer margin requirements for day-trading accounts, many traders have moved away from day trading towards a swing-trading style.

This book — *Swing Trading Simplified* — communicates the essence of Swing Trading in a simple and straightforward manner. It describes the tools necessary to identify swing-trading opportunities, and explains the guidelines needed to implement this strategy. Filled with innovative and important trading techniques, it is a great asset to beginner and experienced swing traders alike.

— Larry Swing
   MrSwing.com

Introduction

It's Time for a
Different Approach

There's little question that making money in the stock market is harder than it used to be. A lot harder!

Throughout most of the 1990s, virtually anyone could be a successful investor. All one had to do was select a stock with the merest hint of promise, buy it and then wait for the surging power of the prolonged bull market to carry its price to the desired target — or beyond. In-depth analysis of a company's fundamentals generally wasn't required prior to purchasing its stock, nor was there a need for excessive concern about timing. Virtually any day was a good day to buy — and, if you missed a good opportunity to sell, there was no reason to fret since a better one would be along shortly.

For those desiring a more proactive approach, "day trading" became the style *du jour*, made possible by the confluence of several key factors. First, the rapidly expanding Internet proved ideal for dissemination of

Throughout most of the 1990s, virtually anyone could be a successful investor. In-depth analysis of a company's fundamentals generally wasn't required prior to purchasing its stock, nor was there a need for excessive concern about timing.

stock prices and related financial information, giving birth, in short order, to the online brokerage industry and the Electronic Communication Networks (ECNs). These technological developments further accelerated the decline in trading costs, which had begun in 1975 when Wall Street first abandoned fixed commissions. The charge for a typical online order fell to pennies a share, with the total cost running as low as $5 for many trades. Thus, for the first time, the individual trader sitting at home in front of his or her PC had access to virtually the same high-quality, real-time market information and order-execution services used by the professional and institutional investors — and commissions were low enough to make short-term, in-and-out stock trading a reasonable fiscal proposition.

Given these newfound advantages, literally tens of thousands of individuals jumped on the day-trading bandwagon, converting from avid amateur investor to intense professional trader. Riding the fairly predictable upward daily price moves within the strongly bullish market, these day traders opened 10, 15 or even 25 positions per day, then closed them out before the final bell for profits as small as 10 or 12 cents per share. And, in the process, many of them rolled up repeated annual gains well into the six-figure range.

In other words, if you were a stock investor — whatever your chosen approach — it was a good time to be alive. *Then everything changed!*

Shortly after calendar page headings started beginning with the numeral "2" (see how cleverly we sidestepped the debate over when the new millennium actually began), the longest bull market in history came to a screeching halt. Suddenly, longer-term investors, who'd been able to buy almost anything and hold it for a profit, instead found almost anything they bought running quickly into the red. Likewise, day traders, who'd come to rely on seeing profitable upward Intra-day moves in virtually every stock, virtually every day, found themselves waiting days on end for a single uptick — an uptick required before they could sell short and thereby profit in the newly bearish climate.

Longer-term investors watched painfully as the plunging market prices cut their portfolio values by a third, then by a half and, finally, for some with heavy concentrations of tech issues, by three-quarters. Underlying values and fundamentals meant little — especially in the face of widespread accounting and management scandals that repeatedly questioned the very truth of those once-sacred appraisals. Day traders also watched their trading opportunities and success rates plummet, initially driving their affordable taste levels from filet mignon status down to hot dog rank, and finally forcing countless numbers of them back to their former non-financial professions.

It was, quite literally, a life-altering shift in market tides.

Then everything changed! Shortly after calendar page headings started beginning with the numeral "2," the longest bull market in history came to a screeching halt. It was, quite literally, a life-altering shift in market tides.

The Other Side of the Coin

Of course, not all market participants found the fledgling century's sudden downturn a devastating experience. Many embraced the new negative sentiment, turning to futures contracts, put options and short-selling strategies to profit from the bearish stock-price moves. Others, who'd been consistently successful during the upward run utilizing a slightly different approach from the longer-term investors and day traders, made modest adjustments to their strategies — and quickly began building a similarly successful record riding the new downward slide.

It's this "slightly different approach" to proven trading success — one that works equally well in both up and down markets — on which this book will focus. It's called "swing trading," and it could be just the dose of medicine you need to restore vitality — and profitability — to your own investment program.

For those unfamiliar with the term, swing trading is sometimes also called "momentum trading" or "position trading." However, we prefer swing trading because that name so closely mirrors the technique's purpose — i.e., it is a strategy designed to exploit short-term stock-price swings. We'll expand on that definition in Chapter 1, but for now just think of swing trading as something of a cross between the quick-in-and-out, low-profit-per-trade approach taken by day traders and the low-frequency, big-gain methodology used by longer-term investors. For example, a swing trader might typically hold a position for three-to-five days, seeking to capture a price move of $1.50 to $3.00 per share.

Note that we've carefully referred to swing trading as a "different approach" to playing the stock market, not a "new" one. That's because swing trading, in one form or another, has been practiced for decades — more than enough time to give the overall concept a well-proven track record. However, the relatively recent advent of electronic analysis, computerized charting and online order processing has turned swing trading into a much more powerful and potentially lucrative strategy—particularly under market conditions like those we're experiencing today.

A Two-Part Learning Approach to Mastering Swing Trading

That's why this book will feature two distinct parts. The first will detail the basic swing-trading concept, as well as providing an overview of the key elements and rules of technical analysis and charting you'll need to understand the strategy and make it work. The second will bring swing trading into the electronic era, discussing a number of proprietary tools developed over the years and then translating these rules into what we call The Master Plan for swinging trading—a plan that's already been profitably used by thousands of successful swing traders. While that instructional line-up might sound a bit intimidating at first, let me assure you that we've taken the advice of Albert Einstein to heart. He said: "Things should be made as simple as possible, but not any simpler."

And that's just what we've done. The rationale behind swing trading is presented clearly and concisely, the analytical foundation gives the basic information you need without a lot of extra technical "mumbo jumbo" and The Master Plan entry and exit rules are spelled out in step-by-step fashion. The result is a simple, practical guide to swing trading that will be an asset for both beginners and experienced market players—a guide that will teach you:

- What swing trading is and why it works
- How to identify stocks to swing trade
- When to initiate a trade

The rationale behind swing trading is presented clearly and concisely, the analytical foundation gives the basic information you need without a lot of extra technical "mumbo jumbo" and The Master Plan entry and exit rules are spelled out in step-by-step fashion.

- When to exit a trade
- How to maximize profits and minimize risk
- Key analytical and online tools you can use to enhance your swing-trading success

With this information, you'll be able to quickly identify and implement your own profitable swing-trading program. And, best of all, you'll be able to do so without having to spend every waking moment glued to your computer monitor. Just open your position, enter a target order to close and a protective stop — and then go back to your normal daily life.

With that assurance, we send you straight ahead to Chapter 1 so you can begin taking the first steps down the path to swing-trading profit.

CHAPTER 1

What It Is—An Overview of the Swing-Trading Concept

Anyone who has watched the market for even a limited period of time knows that stock prices and market indices move up and down. However, they almost never move *straight up* or *straight down*. Instead, they zigzag back and forth, making short swings across a fairly narrow range within a primary longer-term uptrend or downtrend. Those who engage in "swing trading" recognize this fact, and attempt to capitalize on it.

Simply put then, swing trading can be defined as an investment strategy designed to identify and profit from the short-term zigzag price movements that almost always occur within any established market trend. If you can identify the trend and range you can use this knowledge to time market moves and seize profits or cut losses within this range.

A versatile technique, swing trading can be used with equal success in both up and down markets—and, when a specific trading range can be determined, it can also be a profitable strategy with stocks or indices that are essentially moving sideways. Swing trading is

Stock prices and market indices almost never move straight up or straight down—instead, they zigzag back and forth, making short swings across a fairly narrow range within a primary longer-term uptrend or downtrend.

an opportunistic approach to investing, but swing traders are not contrarians. In fact, the astute swing trader will *always* take positions in line with the market's primary direction, living by the axiom, "The trend is your friend." As such, a swing trader's arsenal of strategic options can be broken down into three basic categories:

1. When a stock's primary trend is bullish (i.e., moving upward), the swing trader will monitor for a pullback to the long-term support level and then buy shares, playing for a short-term price rebound to (or beyond) the stock's most recent previous high.

2. When a stock's primary trend is bearish (i.e., moving downward), the swing trader will watch for a rally to the longer-term resistance level and then sell shares short, looking for a near-term pullback to (or below) the stock's most recent previous low.

3. When a stock is range-bound (i.e., locked in a sideways price pattern), the swing trader will either buy on short-term pullbacks to the longer-term support level or sell short on short-term rallies to the longer-term resistance level. Typically, decisions regarding whether to watch for bullish or bearish entry opportunities will be dictated by whether the sideways-moving stock's industry group (or the market as a whole) is tracking in a bullish or bearish pattern.

There are, of course, several additional indicators that can be used to determine the best swing-trading opportunities, as well as some precise guidelines regarding optimum entry and exit points and how to properly allocate your assets to a given trade. Those will be discussed later in this book. For now, however, let's

Why Does Swing Trading Work?

Swing trading is an effective investment tactic because you are always trading in the direction of the primary trend. You wait for a short-term counter-trend move before considering a position, then enter only if the stock gives a clear signal that its price is likely to once again begin moving in the direction of the primary trend.

look a bit more closely at the motivations and objectives of the typical swing trader, once again making a comparison to the longer-term investor and the day trader, as we did briefly in the Introduction.

A Comparison of Trading Styles

Obviously, whether you're a long-term investor, a day trader or a swing trader, your primary goal in initiating any stock position is to make a profit. Beyond that, however, there are significant differences among the three trading styles.

The longer-term (or "buy-and-hold") investor makes only a limited number of trades each year, perhaps as few as five or ten. His strategy is to buy a sizable block of shares, hoping to score a large per-share gain over the course of a fairly lengthy holding period, often up to a year or more. Growth stocks are usually the choice of the investor, and fundamentals tend to weigh heavily in the stock-selection process, with technical analysis used mainly as a timing tool for buy-and-sell decisions. The long-term investor will general-

Whether you're a long-term investor, a day trader or a swing trader, your primary goal in initiating any stock position is to make a profit.

ly tolerate a larger per-share level of risk, giving his stock ample room to fluctuate in price while waiting for the anticipated large move in the desired direction to kick in. Because of the limited number of trades, the total dollar value of the investor's market activity is relatively small compared to that of the day trader or swing trader, and total transaction costs are minimal. An annual return of 25 to 30 percent is an acceptable level of performance for the buy-and-hold investor, with 50 percent considered outstanding.

The longer-term (or "buy-and-hold") investor makes only a limited number of trades — as few as five or ten — *each year*, while the day trader makes 10, 15 or even more round-trip trades of 1,000 or so shares *each day*.

The description of the day-trader's style is the polar opposite of the longer-term investor in almost every respect. The day trader lives a frantic existence, making 10, 15 or even more round-trip trades of 1,000 or so shares each day. He cares nothing for fundamentals, basing his trading decisions almost entirely on ultra-short-term price charts (time segments of five minutes or less). He doesn't need to know anything about the stock other than the direction its price is currently moving, simply because he plans to be out of the trade prior to the closing bell. The day trader can also afford to ignore a company's long-term prospects because he's not looking for a major profit — a move of 25 cents per share or less will usually more than satisfy his objectives. Of course, that also means the day trader has very little room for error; if the price moves against him by even a fraction, he has to bail out immediately. Thus, day trading requires a nerve-wrenching degree of precision and a high percentage of successful trades — an absolute minimum of 60 percent. In addition, because he deals in such a high volume of trades, the day trader has to have a fairly substantial amount of working capital and absorb hefty commission charges. Still, for those who can stand the tension and call short-term market moves accurately, annual returns of 200, 300 or even 400 percent are within the realm of possibility.

Given that this is a book on swing trading, you may be wondering why we've just devoted so much time to explaining the characteristics of two alternate trading styles. There are two reasons. First, it's likely that many of you have tried either day trading or longer-term investing—and are seeking something different based on your less-than-satisfactory results in the recent market environment. Second, the alternative you're looking for could well be swing trading—which, as you've already seen, is something of a "hybrid" strategy featuring the most favorable elements of both day trading and longer-term investing.

Swing trading is something of a "hybrid" strategy featuring the most favorable elements of both day trading and longer-term investing.

The Key Features and Benefits of Swing Trading

The swing trader makes far fewer trades than the day trader, but substantially more than the longer-term investor. Depending on the money management technique used, the swing trader's typical position size also falls somewhere between that of the day trader and buy-and-hold investor. The swing trader's actions are goal driven rather than time driven—unlike the day trader, he has no set time at which he expects to exit his positions, but will wait for a specific price objective to be met. Fortunately, that wait usually isn't too long—typically as little as three to five days, though sometimes as long as two or three weeks.

Swing traders rely almost entirely on technical analysis for entry and exit signals. Entries are triggered when a stock being monitored pulls back to a support level as it fluctuates within a primary bullish trend, or climbs to a resistance level while moving in a primary bearish trend. Profit targets are set based on the width of the stock's recent trading channel within its major trend, and will generally run somewhere from $1.50 to $3.00 per share, depending on the initial price of the stock. The swing trader does need to pay a bit more attention to fundamentals than the day trader, if only to ensure there will be no earnings surprises or other negative reports during the expected holding period. As with the longer-term investor, the swing trader has far more leeway to endure minor adverse price movements early in his trades than does the day trader. He can thus be slightly less precise in his entry timing and utilize slightly more liberal stop-loss limits.

The swing trader will typically follow a large number of stocks, perhaps 20 to 25 issues, and will usually be fully invested, seizing a new opportunity as soon as a former position is closed. As such, a swing trader may make a trade or two every day—but, unlike the day trader, he may also skip a day or two if he is already fully invested or if no new opportunities arise. Because the swing trader turns his portfolio over regularly, his total capital requirement is lower than the long-term investor's, but his commission burden is higher—though it's still far lower than that of the day trader. Swing trading is a proven strategy with fairly clear-cut entry and exit criteria—less demanding than those of the day trader and less subjective than those of the longer-term investor—so it's not difficult to build a strong record of successful trades. As such, annual returns of 50, 100 or even 200 percent are possible for the accomplished swing trader.

> **Swing trading is a proven strategy with fairly clear-cut entry and exit criteria—less demanding than those of the day trader and less subjective than those of the longer-term investor—so it's not difficult to build a strong record of successful trades.**

Why You Should Consider Swing Trading

Potential performance numbers such as those referenced above make swing trading sound like an appealing alternative to other trading styles — but is it really right for you? It's a powerful tool that presents many benefits to today's trader. We can't make that decision for you, but we can offer some questions that will help you determine the road you want your investing future to take:

- **Are you disenchanted with buy-and-hold investing?** More and more people are questioning the merits of this approach — with good reason. Even if you bought shares in really great companies, the value of your investments has most likely fallen substantially over the past few years. While that situation may reverse again in the future, there's no guarantee — but with swing trading, you know you'll be able to make money in both up and down markets.

- **Do you have the expertise needed to be a really good stock analyst?** Even if market conditions do improve in the future, finding and profiting from quality growth issues is no easy task. You need to accurately assess both current values and future prospects for the individual companies, factor in the impact of overall economic conditions — and then hope that nothing unexpected will go wrong while waiting for the best time to sell, assuming you'll eventually be able to determine exactly when that is. With swing trading, it's fairly easy to find good opportunities, the trading period is short and, should you make a mistake, you get

With swing trading, it's fairly easy to find good opportunities, the trading period is short and, should you make a mistake, you get an almost immediate chance to redeem yourself with a new trade.

an almost immediate chance to redeem yourself with a new trade.

- **Do you have the skills and the stomach for day trading, as well as the time to watch the market every minute of every day?** Obviously, day trading requires a very specialized combination of nerves and an ability that most people don't have — or simply don't want to exercise. By contrast, almost anyone can master the art of swing trading — quickly acquiring the necessary knowledge and, without too much effort, developing the discipline and patience required for success. Plus, the time demands are within reason for even busy professionals and you don't need to be locked to a computer screen.

Now that we've highlighted the many positive aspects of swing trading that make it one of today's fastest-growing trading styles, we hope that — with the overall knowledge you'll gain from this book, plus the **Master Plan** rules and other specific guidelines you'll learn — you will quickly be able to launch your own swing-trading program — a program that will enable you to slowly, but surely, increase your wealth using a disciplined, low-risk approach to playing today's uncertain markets.

CHAPTER 2

The Technical Basics of Swing Trading

A s you already know, stock prices nearly always move up and down—but they rarely do so in a straight line. Instead, they track higher or lower in a series of waves that oscillate back and forth within a well-defined trading channel that slopes either up or down, depending on whether the stock is in a bullish or bearish phase. This short-term wave pattern is more than just a function of the investment markets—it's actually nature's preferred pattern for nearly all forms of movement. Light moves in waves. Sound moves in waves. Throw a stone into a pond and the water is displaced in waves, moving outward from the point of impact.

Thus, though the wave patterns found in stock market prices are rarely as uniform as those found in nature (so-called "sine" waves), you can be assured that they do indeed exist—and will continue to exist in the future. This is important because swing-trading profits are entirely dependent on successfully riding these waves—jumping aboard an upward-trending wave pattern when prices are near the bottom of a trough, or climbing on a downward-trending wave

Swing-trading profits are entirely dependent on successfully riding these waves—jumping aboard an upward-trending wave pattern when prices are near the bottom of a trough, or climbing on a downward-trending wave when prices are near the top of a crest.

when prices are near the top of a crest. Given that reality, two questions obviously arise:

1. How do you find stocks that are moving in long-term upward or downward wave patterns (i.e., bullish or bearish primary trends)?

2. How do you define the width of the trading range in which those wave patterns are moving, enabling you to identify when current prices are nearing troughs or crests (i.e., approaching prime entry or exit points)?

In both cases, the answer is the same — *you use technical analysis.*

An Overview of Technical Theory

Technical analysis is one of the two primary methods of evaluating investment opportunities, the other being fundamental analysis. It's probable that most of you already know what technical analysis is, and have a fairly good idea of how it works — at least in theory. However, for those who don't, we'll provide a brief overview, which is all you'll likely need to become a competent swing trader — especially if you avail yourself of one of the many fine technical analysis software packages or online advisory services currently on the market, many of which are highlighted later in the book. Then, we'll discuss some specific technical indicators that are most helpful in finding top swing-trading opportunities and making entry and exit decisions.

First, a glance at fundamental analysis, which might really be considered the search for hidden value in a potential investment. Very briefly, fundamental analysis involves evaluating a company on the basis of its

Fundamental analysis involves evaluating a company on the basis of its revenues, balance sheet, products, production capacity, market demand, etc., then factoring in the overall economic climate, in order to arrive at a projection of its potential earnings growth and, by association, its future stock price.

revenues, balance sheet, products, production capacity, market demand, etc., then factoring in the overall economic climate, in order to arrive at a projection of its potential earnings growth and, by association, its future stock price.

By contrast, technical analysis assumes the market knows all the key fundamental information about a company before it becomes public and factors that information into the present price. The technician seeks to interpret the market reaction to this information by analyzing price movements as they are depicted in various chart patterns, then predict future price action based on how similar patterns evolved in the past.

Technical analysis can best be described as the study of historical price performance in an effort to predict future price movements.

In short, then, technical analysis can best be described as the study of historical price performance in an effort to predict future price movements.

Why Price Is So Important

The technician's focus on price is justified because price is the only truly accurate measure of investor sentiment — it is the meeting point of supply and demand for every investment. However, the technical assessment of price is not quite as simple as it might seem, the result of three important considerations:

- First, contrary to some widely touted theories, price is *not* random. Some critics of technical analysis agree that price is the end result of everything known about a particular security at any given time. However, they claim this body of knowledge is constantly changing, so it's impossible to predict price with any degree of success. Their assertion is that price is random. However, if you look at price charts objectively, it quickly becomes apparent that this contention is flawed. Prices clearly do not move in random fashion, but rather experience periods of consolidation, when supply and demand is in relative balance, as well as periods featuring rapid price change (or trends), resulting from an imbalance between supply and demand.

Three key points to remember about stock prices are:
1. Price is not random.
2. Although price is the sum of present knowledge about an investment, it's not really reactive — rather, it anticipates changes in fundamentals.
3. There is a linear relationship between price and time.

- Second, although price is the sum of present knowledge about an investment, it's not really reactive. Rather, it anticipates changes in fundamentals. Corporate fundamentals usually don't change overnight — they shift gradually. But, while price is indeed a factor of all knowledge about a stock, both public and private, some buyers and sellers are more informed than others — the so-called "smart money." It is buying or selling by these better-informed smart-money players that anticipates fundamental changes and creates price trends. While this smart-money advantage may seem unfair, it is a fact of life. Information is a commodity, like any other, and those with greater resources have more access to that commodity. Keep this in mind whenever you encounter a stock that seems to be rising or falling without any publicly apparent reason.

- Third, there is a linear relationship between price and time. This is one of the most difficult concepts for fledgling technicians to grasp. What it essentially means, however, is that the longer a stock's price fails to behave as expected, the more likely investors will become to revise their perception of the stock's fair value. A simple example of this involves the purchase of a stock that immediately goes down instead of up. Since most investors don't like to take losses, they tend to hold longer than they should, hoping for a rebound that will get them out with at least a break-even. However, as more and more time passes, the investor eventually revises his perception of the stock's value and changes his opinion regarding an adequate exit price. In addition, this linear relationship between time and price is exponential—i.e., the longer the time frame stretches, the more elastic price expectations become. That's why breakouts from a prolonged base-building (or consolidation) period tend to be much stronger than those that merely penetrate an already rising trend line.

We've taken the time to stress these three points because they all help explain why stock prices tend to move in trends—as well as why they typically break out of those trends or unexpectedly reverse. And, as you've already learned, it is trading in conjunction with major price trends that helps make swing trading such a potentially profitable technique.

We've taken the time to stress these three points because they all help explain why stock prices tend to move in trends—as well as why they typically break out of those trends or unexpectedly reverse.

Support and Resistance—Two Key Technical Concepts

You've also learned that swing trading involves playing the shorter-term back-and-forth action of prices within those primary trends—which raises one additional obvious question: How do you determine the upper and lower boundaries of that back-and-forth price action?

The answer relates to the final two important concepts in our overview of technical analysis—support and resistance.

Support and resistance are among the cornerstone precepts of technical analysis, and a clear understanding of them is vital because they are the defining factors in most swing trading entry and exit decisions. Fortunately, they are not difficult ideas to grasp. To wit:

- **Support** is the price level at which traders have historically shown *a willingness to purchase* a given stock or security.

- **Resistance** is the price level at which traders have historically shown *a willingness to sell* a given stock or security.

These definitions may seem a bit simplistic, but they're accurate because, in very many cases, price is ultimately governed by basic human emotions. For example, we've all been in the position of buying a stock and immediately having it start to decline. Our initial instinct is to resist selling the stock until it rebounds by enough that we can do so without taking a loss. If enough other people bought at the same price as we did and subsequently suffered the same "buyer's remorse," then that price will become a "resistance level" — simply because investors eager to "at least break even" will sell each time the stock reaches that point. Resistance points often develop after a stock has had a lengthy advance ahead of a key news event. As traders "sell on the news," some unlucky investors are "trapped" by an absence of new buyers. That leads to weakness, and the stock begins to fall. Subsequently, each time the stock rallies to that same level, those unhappy with their earlier purchase will sell.

In slightly different terms then, *a resistance level can be defined as the price point at which the supply of a stock exceeds the demand for it.*

Support is a bit more difficult to illustrate. A support level usually develops as a result of traders being rewarded for purchasing a stock at a specific price. If you buy a stock at a given price level and it immediately rallies, odds are you will feel good about both yourself and your purchase price. Once you sell that stock at a profit, you're likely to consider buying it again should it pull back to that same price. (Hey, it worked once. Why shouldn't it work again?) If enough investors share your sentiment and are willing to buy at that same price, then that price becomes a support level.

Once again phrasing it in a slightly different way, *a support level can be defined as the price point at which the demand for a stock will exceed its supply.*

One additional key point: Support and resistance levels may **not** be static over time — i.e., the line depicting them on a price chart **may not be flat**.

If a stock is in a consolidation (or base-building) phase, then both support and resistance levels will remain roughly the same (and the lines showing them on a chart will be essentially flat) until there is a price breakout in one direction or the other. However, that's not the case if a stock is trending either up or down. When a stock is in an uptrend, the support level will rise each time the low on a short-term price swing is higher than the last previous short-term low — and the resistance level will rise each time the high on a short-term price swing is higher than the last previous short-term high. The chart lines depicting both support and resistance levels will thus have an upward slant (moving from left to right). Likewise, when a

A resistance level can be defined as the price point at which the supply of a stock exceeds the demand for it. A support level can be defined as the price point at which the demand for a stock will exceed its supply.

Understanding the nuances of support and resistance, and learning to recognize the specific levels for each on the price chart of a given stock, is perhaps the most important element in becoming a successful swing trader.

stock is in a downtrend, the support level will fall each time the low on a short-term price swing is lower than the last previous short-term low—and the resistance level will decline each time the high on a short-term price swing is lower than the last previous short-term high. In a downtrend then, the chart lines depicting both support and resistance levels will have an downward slant (again moving from left to right).

Understanding the nuances of support and resistance, and learning to recognize the specific levels for each on the price chart of a given stock, is perhaps the most important element in becoming a successful swing trader—which is why we're now going to turn our attention to the subject of charting.

CHAPTER 3

Recognizing Key Trend Patterns

Most humans have a very hard time interpreting an assortment of complicated investment data with the speed necessary to make efficient market decisions. That is why, as human stock traders, we strive to find ways of presenting such data in a manner that makes it easier to analyze. Perhaps the most effective means of doing that is through the use of stock charts—which can, in a matter of minutes, convey the information needed to identify quality trading opportunities and suggest optimum price points for seizing those opportunities.

There are, of course, several different kinds of charts, and the list of the various types of indicators they can be adapted to display is virtually endless. However, regardless of the style, all charts do essentially the same thing—they provide a visual representation of the results of technical analysis, recapping the historical price action of the security being analyzed. Even the simplest of charts can provide a wealth of information. Take, for example, the basic line chart of General Electric Co. (GE) shown in Figure 3.1 on the next page. Although it features just three lines—the price line, a 50-day moving average (MA) line and a 200-day moving average line—you can tell a lot about GE with even the quickest glance. To wit, it had been in a

Most traders and investors pay attention only to price movements, ignoring trading volume. Gann believed that trading success hinged on being able to put the two together into one comprehensive picture to be able to interpret the balance of supply and demand in a given stock or commodity.

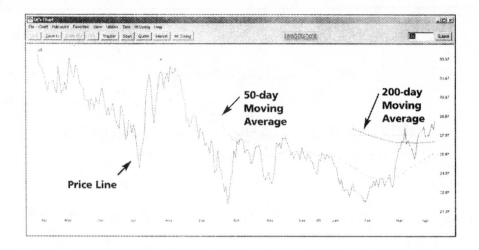

FIGURE 3-1:
One-year Line
Chart of GE stock
featuring a
50-day and 200-
day moving
average.

steady downward trend for the better part of a year —
then, in March 2003, it staged a sharp upward breakout, penetrating first the 50-day MA and, a few days
later, the 200-day MA, before pulling back slightly.
That was a very bullish move and, if the pullback held
above the 200-day MA line, most likely signaled a
reversal and the start of a new upward trend.

We tell you that not to suggest that GE is a good
swing-trading candidate, or a good investment in general, but merely to demonstrate the power that even
a simple chart has in providing insight into the psychology of the market. That's important because psychology is one of the most important elements of
technical analysis. In fact, what technicians actually do
is trade people, not stocks. That's a key reason technical analysis is so successful in forecasting future price
movements — because people never change! They
keep making the same investment mistakes over and
over — which is a lucky thing for those of us who
hope to profit from such mistakes.

Selecting the Best Charts for Swing Trading

Charts become even more powerful tools as their format is changed or new indicators are added. Figure 3.2 simply, yet clearly, illustrates this. It covers the same one-year trading period for General Electric stock, with the same moving averages. This time, however, rather than illustrating the price with a single line, the chart features a bar for each trading day — a so-called "candlestick" that shows the opening and closing prices, as well as the range of prices covered during the course of that day's trading. This gives the analyst further information about the direction of emerging trends, as well as the strength of price moves contributing to those trends. The top portion of this chart also features a series of bars illustrating the trading volume experienced each day — also very important as

FIGURE 3-2: One-year chart of GE stock featuring a 50-day and 200-day moving average.

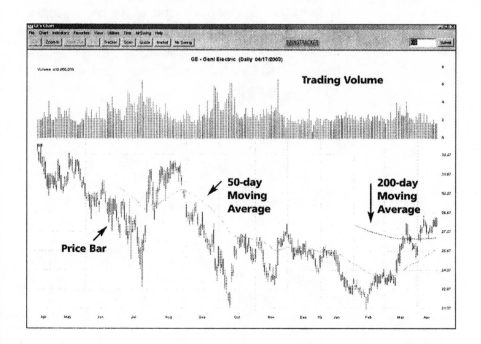

Volume Bars

Volume is simply the number of shares of a stock traded during a given time period.

volume provides key clues regarding the intensity of a given price move. (Volume numbers also reveal institutional interest in a particular stock, since large professional traders can't help but leave behind "footprints" pointing in the direction they think prices are heading.)

As noted, the two charts already shown are representative of the most simple charting methodology used. Once you become more deeply involved in swing trading and hone your analytical skills, you'll want to advance to more sophisticated chart types that convey added information. In fact, even if you don't do any of your own charting or analysis, but instead use an on-line service such as MasterSwings or others in the market, you will still need to be familiar with the more advanced chart types as virtually all the top analysts and advisors use them. Thus, to help you ramp up your learning curve, we'll take a little extra time here to familiarize you with a couple of the most popular charting forms, with a focus on those most appropriate for swing-trading applications and those embraced by some of the most widely known professional swing traders.

A Look at Japanese Candlesticks

One of the most popular charting formats involves the use of "Japanese candlesticks," so called because they were first developed in the 1600s by Japanese traders, who used them to chart the prices of rice contracts. Their use in this country was popularized by an analyst named Steven Nison, who is now considered the leading expert on their interpretation. Thanks to his efforts—coupled with the clarity with which they illustrate price movements—candlestick charts have

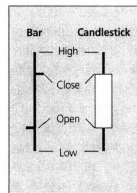

The bar chart displays the opening, closing, high and low prices on a vertical bar that joins the high and low prices. Opening and closing prices are shown as small horizontal ticks at the side of the bar, and no distinction is made between up and down price moves. The candlestick displays the highs and lows as the ends of a "real body," with highs and lows shown as additional vertical lines extended from that body. A clear distinction is made between up and down moves. Up moves have a clear (or white) real body; down moves have a black (or colored) real body. The open and close are the key points.

now become so popular in the West that the term "Japanese" has generally been dropped from the name.

As with the standard bar chart, candlestick charts display the open, high, low and closing prices for each day's price action in a given stock or market index. However, they do so in a manner that accentuates the relationship between the opening and closing prices. Figure 3.3, above, illustrates the key differences.

As you can see, bullish candlesticks have a "real body" that appears clear or white. Had the day's trading action been bearish — i.e., with the open higher than the close — the "real body" of the candlestick would have been solid, or black. (Note: Some computer candlestick charting programs use green bodies for up moves and red bodies for down days.) The thinner line extending from the top of the body to the day's high is called the upper "shadow," while the line extending from the bottom of the body to the day's low is known as the lower "shadow." The "real bodies" and differing colors with which they are filled provide a far more dramatic presentation of a given day's price movement than does the basic bar chart.

FIGURE 3.3
The two figures above illustrate a typical bar chart symbol and a candlestick symbol for the same trading day.

Far Eastern traders have used candlestick charts to track stock market activity for more than a century. Working with that huge base of market data, Eastern analysts have identified a number of candlestick patterns that, with differing degrees of reliability, can help determine the future short-term trend for a particular investment, based on what the charts reveal regarding the psychology of the market at a given time. In other words, based on a particular pattern, an investor can make confident decisions about buying, selling or holding the underlying stock.

FIGURE 3-4: Three-month Candlestick Chart of GE stock featuring a 50-day and 200-day moving average.

Just so you can begin getting a feel for how candlestick charts look — and compare them to line and bar charts — Figure 3.4, below, shows the final three months of the trading pattern for General Electric Co.

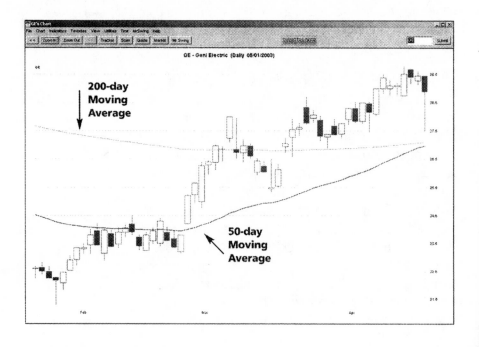

that was featured in Figures 3.1 and 3.2. Note how clearly the different colors filling the real bodies illustrate the stock's bullish breakout (white candlesticks) from its long basing pattern.

Some Key Candlestick Charting Terminology

Following are some additional terms used in candlestick charting and analysis that you may encounter as you become more involved in swing trading and the use of these charts in seeking out prime trade opportunities.

Long Day—A candlestick has a long day when there is a large difference between opening and closing prices when compared to other trading days in the prior five- to ten-day period.

Short Day—A candlestick has a short day when there is a small difference between opening and closing prices relative to typical trading days in the previous five- to ten-day period.

Marubozu—A marubozu candlestick is one that exhibits very little (or no) upper or lower shadow. For a white (bullish) candlestick, this means the open is roughly equal to the low, and the close is about equal to the high. For a black (bearish) candlestick, it means that the open is right at the high, and the close is essentially equal to the low.

Spinning Top—A spinning top is a candlestick with a very small real body, but with long upper and lower shadows.

Doji — A doji is the most extreme case of a spinning top. It occurs when the real body is simply a line (i.e., the day's open and close are the same). A long-legged doji has extended upper and lower shadows. A gravestone doji has a long upper shadow and no lower shadow. A dragonfly doji has no upper shadow, but an extended lower shadow. And, finally, a four-price doji has no upper or lower shadows — i.e., the open, high, low and close are all the same.

Star — A star is a candlestick with small real body gapping above or below a long candlestick that occurred the previous trading day.

Umbrella and Inverted Umbrella — An umbrella is similar to a dragonfly doji, having a small real body, with no upper shadow but a long lower shadow. An inverted umbrella is similar to a gravestone doji, having a small real body with a long upper shadow but no lower shadow.

Indicator — An indicator is a group of candlesticks (from two to as many as five) that meet a set of pre-determined criteria. These criteria may include prior trend, real body length, shadow length, long and short days, opening and closing gaps, etc. Indicators are generally considered to signal bullish or bearish trends and/or patterns associated with those trends (reversal or continuation) that are likely to continue for the short term.

Pattern — In candlestick charting, an indicator always has a pattern associated with it. This could be a "continuation pattern," meaning a stock that is in a bullish trend should continue to stay bullish, or a stock that is in a bearish trend should continue to stay bearish. It could also be a "reversal pattern," meaning a stock that is currently bullish will likely turn bearish, or a stock that is presently bearish is likely to turn bullish.

Reliability—This is a term loosely used to classify how good a job an indicator does at determining the short-term price outlook of a stock. Some indicators are, of course, more reliable than others—for example, those that take three or more days to develop or that have strong candlesticks (such as marubozus or stars) tend to have higher success rates.

The Biggest Flaw With Candlesticks

Although they are intriguing and frequently very useful, candlesticks are really just a different way of looking at price—i.e., they don't involve any calculations. In addition, they have one significant flaw—they don't make any allowance for or provide any illustration of volume.

For those unsure of the precise definition, volume is simply the number of shares of a stock traded during a given time period—e.g., within an hour, a day, a week, a month, etc. The analysis of volume is a basic, but very important component of technical analysis, providing significant clues as to the strength or weakness of a given price move. For example, high volume levels are a characteristic of market tops when there is a strong consensus that prices will continue moving higher. High volume is also very common at the beginning of new trends—i.e., when prices break out of a trading range. Volume will also often increase dramatically just before market bottoms, the result of panic-driven selling.

Volume is an extremely useful tool for swing traders because it can help determine the strength of an existing trend. Specifically, a strong uptrend should have higher volume on the short-term upward waves, and

The analysis of volume is a basic, but very important component of technical analysis, providing significant clues as to the strength or weakness of a given price move.

lower volume on the minor downward (corrective) waves. Similarly, strong downtrends have higher volume on the minor downward legs and lower volume on the short-term upward (corrective) legs. If that is not the case, it's frequently a sign that the primary trend is losing strength and a reversal may be on the near horizon.

Adding Volume to the Candlestick Equation

What makes Equivolume unique is the *width* of the candlestick's real body. It varies depending on the level of volume during the covered trading period— the greater the volume, the wider the body, and vice versa.

Because volume is such an important element in selecting prime swing-trading opportunities, we prefer a slightly modified variation of candlestick charting known as "Equivolume."

Equivolume displays candlestick patterns in a manner that emphasizes the relationship between price and volume. It was developed by Richard W. Arms, Jr., and is explained in greater detail in his book, *Volume Cycles in the Stock Market*. Instead of displaying volume as an "afterthought" on the lower margin of a bar or candlestick chart, Equivolume actually integrates volume into the "real body" of the candlestick, giving it a second dimension—i.e., width, as well as length.

As in standard candlestick charting, the top line of the candlestick body represents either the open or close for the trading period, depending on whether it's a bearish or bullish day, with the bottom line reflecting the opposite. Shadows again extend above and below the real body to the point of the daily high and daily low, respectively. What makes Equivolume unique is the *width* of the candlestick's real body. It varies depending on the level of volume during the covered trading period—the greater the volume, the wider

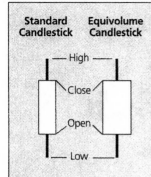

Standard Candlestick **Equivolume Candlestick** The two figures at the left illustrate a standard bullish candlestick line (left) and one modified with the Equivolume feature (right). The "real body" of the Equivolume version tells the technical analyst that trading volume on this particular day was heavier than normal, while a very narrow box would indicate a day with lighter-than-usual trading volume. An algorithm devised by Equivolume's creator determines the relative width of the day-to-day boxes, based on the actual volume levels. You'll see several examples of Equivolume charts later that will clearly demonstrate the value of this added feature.

the body, and vice versa. Figure 3.5, above, illustrates this more clearly.

The shape of each Equivolume box provides a picture of the supply and demand for the covered stock during a specific trading period. For example, short and wide boxes indicate days of heavy volume but small changes in prices, which tend to occur at turning points. Conversely, tall and narrow boxes reflect light volume accompanied by large changes in price — conditions that are more likely to occur when the stock is trading in an established trend. Especially important are wide boxes that penetrate support or resistance levels since heavy volume serves to confirm penetrations.

A "power box" is one in which both height and width increase substantially, reflecting both a large price change and heavy volume. Power boxes provide excellent confirmation of a possible breakout. By contrast, a possible breakout is highly suspect if its Equivolume box is long and narrow since there was little volume to support the large price change.

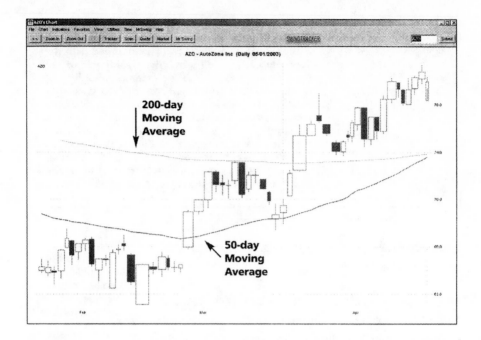

FIGURE 3.6 Equivolume Candlestick Chart for Autozone, Inc. (AZO).

The chart for Autozone, Inc. (AZO), shown in Figure 3.6, illustrates a variety of Equivolume candlestick boxes.

Volume as a Key Component of Trend Analysis

I recommend looking at volume in relation to price movement, simply because the two in combination help to both establish trends and provide signals regarding whether they are likely to continue or move into a reversal phase. And, as we've repeatedly stressed, it is the process of trading short-term waves within longer-term trends that makes swing trading such a powerful investment technique. Review the information in the box on the following page, which defines the distinct price-volume relationships that

Volume-Price Relationships Affecting Trend Performance

Trend Reversals are typically signaled by:
- **Above**-average volume with very **little** price movement.
- **Above**-average volume that follows a **strong** advance or decline in prices.

Trend Continuation is typically signaled by:
- **Above**-average volume with very **strong** price movement.
- **Above**-average volume in conjunction with a price **breakout.**
- **Below**-average volume with **NO** price movement.

I recommend looking at volume in relation to price movement, simply because the two in combination help to both establish trends and provide signals regarding whether they are likely to continue or move into a reversal phase.

accompany both trend reversal and trend continuation signals. Then, we'll conclude this chapter by taking a quick look at two examples of actual trend patterns — just so you'll have the pictures clear in your mind when we finally begin discussing the specific elements of our swing-trading **Master Plan.**

Let's Look at an Uptrend

Although they've been relatively rare in the early part of the 21st century, most swing traders prefer to operate within uptrends — simply because they feel more comfortable buying stocks than selling them short. So, let's begin our look at trends with an example of one heading in an upward direction.

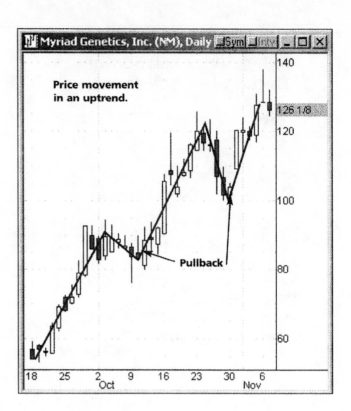

FIGURE 3.7
This standard candlestick chart shows the price movement for Myriad Genetics, Inc. (MYGN) in an uptrend.

The candlestick chart in Figure 3.7, above, shows the price movement of Myriad Genetics (MYGN) in an established uptrend. Note that the upward movement does not take place in a straight line — or even a uniform zigzag pattern. Rather, it moves upward until short-term demand is exhausted, then it pulls back, or takes a rest, until it reaches a time — or, more frequently, a price level — when demand once again kicks in. Indeed, the resurgence of demand usually occurs at a specific price level, with the actual duration of the pullback determined by how long it takes the price to ease back to that level. If it pulls back fairly slowly, the "zag" will have a shallow slant (as does the first one in the MYGN chart), but if a large price drop occurs quickly, the angle of the "zag" will be fairly steep (the case with the second MYGN pullback).

Understanding the mechanics of the price pullbacks is important because, when we swing trade in an uptrend, we buy **only on a pullback.**

As should show clearly in an established chart, an uptrend can be identified by an alternating progression of higher short-term highs and lower short-term lows. In other words, an uptrend is a series of successive minor rallies, with each rally going higher than the previous one, interrupted by successive minor pullbacks, the bottom of each stopping at a higher level than the prior one. As noted above, the zigzag pattern typically won't be perfectly uniform, looking more like the erose edge of a saw blade than a sinusoid.

Nonetheless, once the uptrend is established, the price pattern tends to repeat itself — an important fact since, in swing trading, we capitalize on the predictability of the pattern. By buying only on pullbacks that offer the proven expectation of a subsequent rally, we greatly increase our chances of making a profit.

Understanding the mechanics of the price pullbacks is important because, when we swing trade in an uptrend, we buy only on a pullback.

By buying only on pullbacks that offer the proven expectation of a subsequent rally, we greatly increase our chances of making a profit.

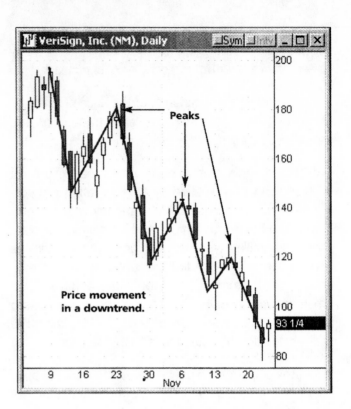

FIGURE 3.8
This standard candlestick chart shows the price movement for VeriSign, Inc. (VRSN) in a downtrend.

Now Let's Look at a Downtrend

The standard candlestick chart in Figure 3.8, above, shows the price movement of VeriSign, Inc. (VRSN), in an established downtrend. As with the uptrend discussed earlier, the VeriSign decline doesn't take place in a straight line. Instead, the price moves down until the short-term selling pressure (supply) is exhausted, then rebounds until it reaches a price point at which renewed selling interest develops. Again, we have a zigzag pattern, albeit one that is irregular rather than uniform.

Applying the same terminology as before, a down-trend can thus be identified as a progression of minor pullbacks, with each decline falling lower than the previous low, separated by a series of minor rallies, with the top (or peak) of each stopping at a lower level than the previous one. Again, the repetition of this pattern is important because, when we swing trade in a downtrend, we sell short *only near the peaks of the minor rallies* — with the proven expectation of a subsequent pullback once more boosting our chances of making a profit.

When we swing trade in a down-trend, we sell short only near the peaks of the minor rallies— with the proven expectation of a subsequent pullback once more boosting our chances of making a profit.

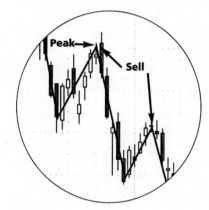

When we swing trade in a downtrend, we sell short only near the peaks of the minor rallies.

CHAPTER 4

How to Develop a
Swing-Trading Master Plan

B uilding on the background provided in Chapters
1, 2 and 3, we're now going to walk you through
the actual steps you'll need to begin swing trading on your own. Then, once you are clear on the overall process, we will detail the precise rules we recommend you follow in entering and exiting your swing
trade positions—our so-called **Master Plan**.

Start by Getting Your Account in Order

Once you decide you want to try your hand at swing
trading, the very first step you must take is to open an
account with an online broker—preferably one that
offers a substantial commission discount relative to
regular full-service brokers. This is essential because,
depending on your level of capital commitment and
the universe of stocks you choose to follow, you may
be making five, six or even more round-trip trades per
week—which means commission costs can mount
up very quickly, even if you're getting a preferred rate.
(A list of online discount brokers is featured later in

**Once you decide
you want to try
your hand at
swing trading,
the very first
step you must
take is to open
an account
with an online
broker—prefer-
ably one that
offers a substan-
tial commission
discount relative
to regular full-
service brokers.**

the book, along with some specifics regarding a couple of our preferred choices—just for the sake of comparison.)

When setting up your online account, be sure that you are approved for "margin" trading, which is required before you will be permitted to sell stocks short—a key component of any successful swing-trading program. At the same time, you may want to take a few moments and consider whether you actually want to trade "on margin"—i.e., borrowing a portion (usually 50 percent) of the price of the stocks you buy from your broker.

Trading on margin means borrowing a portion (usually 50 percent) of the price of the stocks you buy from your broker.

Buying on margin has its advantages—e.g., it increases your leverage, boosts your overall buying power and allows you to seize more opportunities—but it also has some drawbacks. For starters, there are costs involved (interest on the borrowed funds), plus holding stocks on margin can put you under substantial added pressure. To wit, if the price of a margined stock moves against you, you may be forced to put up additional money or, if you don't have the money to put up, to close out your position at a less-than-desirable price.

This is the impetus for many steep market declines. The trading day will begin with a pullback that, though modest, is large enough to trigger some "margin calls." Lacking liquidity, the traders receiving those calls are forced to sell some of their shares, which drives prices down further, triggering still more margin calls—and the cycle feeds on itself until a full-fledged free-fall is under way. (This same situation in reverse—a so-called "short squeeze"—will sometimes also trigger a sizable market rally.)

The decision as to whether you want to trade on margin must be a personal one — not knowing your individual financial situation or your emotional tolerance for risk, we can't make it for you. However, as we said, to swing trade, you do need to have a margin account, even if you plan never to trade "on margin."

A Word About Money Management

There are also some other details you'll want to check on when opening your account, primarily related to money management and the manner in which the brokerage firm allocates your funds. For starters, you should ensure that your account has a so-called "sweep" feature — i.e., that any funds not committed to open trades are automatically swept into a money market account at the end of the day so they earn interest (though the impact of that will obviously be minimal in today's interest-rate environment).

Beyond that, you need to be aware that good money management is extremely important in swing trading. You don't want to allocate too large a percentage of your trading capital to a single position, as that unnecessarily increases your overall level of risk. Likewise, you don't want to spread your capital across too many trades, as that could reduce the size of your individual positions to the point that any single profit becomes almost insignificant. This would put too much pressure on you to be right, requiring you to make a profit on almost every trade in order to manage an adequate overall return.

As you become more experienced you'll find an equation that works for you. The well-known swing trader "Mr. Swing" personally divides his trading capital by

> **Sweep feature means that any funds not committed to open trades are automatically swept into a money market account at the end of the day so they earn interest.**

15 and then commits that amount to each individual trade. As he takes profits and the total size of his account grows, so too does the amount he allocates to each individual trade. How you allocate your capital will, of course, depend on how much you have. If you are starting small, you may want to limit yourself to three or four trades at a time — keeping your trade size the same, but adding more positions as profits from your early trades increase the size of your account. If you're comfortable committing more funds to swing trading, you may want to target having 10, 15 or even 20 trades open at one time (although most people find it difficult to manage more than about 15 positions at once).

If you plan to be an active swing trader, you need to make sure, up front, that your account is set up so that once the available capital is used up, the broker will automatically cancel the rest of the open orders.

Whatever number you pick, you need to ensure in advance that your account will accommodate the trading style you choose. For example, Mr. Swing identifies 20 to 25 candidates for new swing trades each day. However, if he already has, say, 10 positions open, that means he only has enough available capital for five new trades. So, he picks the 10 best candidates from a list of 25 — then places orders for all of them. Some of the orders won't get filled due to price action, but others will — and, as soon as there are five fills, using up all available capital, the broker will automatically cancel the rest of the open orders. That way there's no worry about running out of money — or committing more funds than available. I explain all this because, if you plan to be an active swing trader, you need to make sure, up front, that your account works this way. Otherwise, your brokerage firm might fill every order you put in — and then expect you to come up with the added cash within the next few days.

Building Your List of Swing-Trading Candidates

Once your account is in order, you're ready to take the first step toward becoming an active swing trader, and that means assembling a universe of stocks to monitor for entry opportunities. Theoretically, since all stocks are priced in the same manner and trade essentially the same way, almost any group of stocks should do. However, common sense dictates that a few guidelines are in order.

For starters, since swing trading requires buying and selling stocks that do, in fact, *swing* a fair amount in price, you need to start with stocks that demonstrate a reasonable degree of volatility. Nearly all analytical software programs track some measure of volatility—usually the so-called *Beta* coefficient, which gauges how much an individual stock moves, in price, relative to movement in the S&P 500 Index. For example, a stock with a Beta of 1.0 is considered to be equivalent to the S&P 500, so one with a Beta of 1.5 would be 50 percent more volatile than the index, whereas one with a Beta of 0.5 would move just half as much. As a rough rule of thumb then, you should probably restrict your list of swing-trading candidates to stocks with *a Beta of 1.3 or greater*—which will include a lot of growth and technology issues.

In addition to volatility, your candidate stocks need to have a reasonably wide absolute-trading range. After all, even a stock that gyrates a lot won't give you much opportunity for profitable trades if the range between its annual high and low is only $3 or $4 a share (which is the case with some utilities and high-dividend financial issues). Similarly, you need to stick

Since swing trading requires buying and selling stocks that do, in fact, *swing* a fair amount in price, you need to start with stocks that :
- **demonstrate a reasonable degree of volatility**
- **have a reasonably wide absolute-trading range**
- **have a hefty daily trading volume**

with stocks that have a decent price level to begin with. Again, even if a stock priced at $5 a share is fairly volatile, it's unlikely to move more than 25 to 50 cents in a single day, or $1 to $2 a share in a week. That means even perfectly timed swing trades won't generate that much profit. Thus, we recommend you track only stocks with a *current price of $12 or more* and a minimum *average absolute trading range of $3 to $5 per week.*

Finally, you want to stick to stocks that have a hefty daily trading volume. It does you no good to find a volatile stock with a wide range between high and low prices if that stock trades only a few thousand shares a day. You'll simply have too much difficulty opening and closing your trades at the prices you want, plus you may have trouble buying enough shares to fulfill your money-management guidelines —i.e., enough shares to generate a reasonable profit if the trade's a success. Thus, we suggest you monitor only those stocks with an average *daily volume of at least 500,000 shares.*

The box on the next page summarizes these guidelines regarding appropriate stocks to include among your candidates for swing-trading opportunities. Remember, too, that you don't personally have to hunt down the specific information for each stock. Every good technical analysis software package has a "screening" function that lets you enter your desired criteria, then runs them against a list of all available stocks to determine which ones fulfill the conditions you've set. Most quality advisory services also offer screening tools, as well as providing tips on how to refine your search criteria and fine-tune your selection process.

Every good technical analysis software package has a "screening" function that lets you enter your desired criteria, then runs them against a list of all available stocks to determine which ones fulfill the conditions you've set.

The Steps Involved in Swing Trading

Once you've put together a list of stocks to monitor for swing-trading opportunities, the process of actually identifying and executing your first swing trades is really quite simple. There are only five basic steps:

Step 1 — From your list of trading candidates, identify those stocks that are currently in an established trend, either upward or downward.

Step 2 — From the stocks that are in an established uptrend, pick out those that are currently experiencing a pullback. Similarly, among the stocks in an established downtrend, identify those currently staging a short-term rally.

Step 3 — Choose the most attractive prospects — i.e., those that appear to be coming out of their short-term pullback or coming off the peak of their short-term rally — and place limit orders to open your positions, based on the specific rules featured in the

Master Plan, which you'll learn about in just a few minutes. Remember, you want to *buy* stocks that are in an established *uptrend* and *sell short* stocks that are in a primary *downtrend*.

Step 4 — Once you've successfully opened a long or short position, place a stop-loss order to protect yourself against an adverse price move, as well as a limit order to close the position at the price needed to produce your desired profit. Ideally, your broker will allow you to place these two orders at the same time on an OCO (One Cancels Other) or OCA (One Cancels All) basis.

Step 5 — At the end of each trading day, adjust your stop-loss order prices based on the guidelines that will be spelled out in the Master Plan.

A Couple of Notes on What to Expect

Swing trading through an online broker has some distinct differences from other trading methodologies, so it's likely you may encounter some things you don't expect. Here are a couple of added notes that may help you avoid some confusion as you're getting started. Review them quickly; then we'll move ahead and give you the specific rules featured in our swing-trading Master Plan.

First, don't be disappointed when some of your orders to initiate swing trades don't get filled. Remember, you will be using limit orders only. If such an order doesn't get filled, it's because the market moved the opposite of what you expected — meaning you didn't want the position anyway. In fact, the rules set out in the Master Plan are specifically designed to allow entry

Remember, you want to *buy* stocks that are in an established *uptrend* and *sell short* stocks that are in a primary *downtrend*.

only when the price of the target stock moves in the anticipated direction; if it doesn't, entry to the trade won't be possible.

If you're accustomed to the long-term, buy-and-hold style of investing, you may at first find it difficult to exit your positions as soon as your target is reached. The tendency of most people is to hold onto a position until they receive some negative signal, usually a price reversal — which may be either so subtle or so sudden that it wipes out a big chunk of your profit from the prior move. Swing trading's purpose is to avoid exactly such situations by identifying the size of a likely move in advance (based on the width of the trading range within the primary trend), then grabbing the target profit as soon as it's achieved. And, once that profit is taken, the swing trader never wastes time worrying that he or she acted too soon — instead focusing on finding the next opportunity and repeating the entire profitable process.

In spite of the overwhelming tendency of trends to continue, and the carefully thought-out rules we've devised for playing swings within those trends, some of your trades will result in losses. However, if you religiously follow the stop-loss guidelines detailed in the Master Plan, adjusting your protective orders as the price moves in your favor (a so-called "trailing" stop), such losses will be minimized. Exercise precision and patience in choosing the best entry opportunities, plus discipline in adhering to the exit guidelines and loss limits, and your profitable trades will almost certainly far outnumber your losing endeavors — meaning you *will* make money in the long run.

Now, let's find out exactly what's in this Master Plan we've been talking about.

Swing trading's purpose is to avoid exactly such situations by identifying the size of a likely move in advance (based on the width of the trading range within the primary trend), then grabbing the target profit as soon as it's achieved.

Entry and Exit Rules To Ensure Swing-Trading Success

As you've no doubt surmised by now, the Master Plan is a set of rules spelling out exactly when and under what conditions you should enter and exit your swing trades. When you first read these rules, they may seem somewhat complicated. However, once you've placed a few trades, you'll realize it's really quite simple. The best characteristic of the Master Plan is that it doesn't require you to use your own judgment—the rules are entirely mechanical. Although your initial reaction to this might be negative, further thought should convince you it's actually a major advantage. Here's why. The two biggest obstacles to success in trading are human emotions—specifically, fear and greed. But, when you follow a mechanical system like that spelled out in the Master Plan, you take emotions out of the equation. They don't influence your investment actions—and thus, can't negatively impact your profits.

The Master Plan is a set of rules spelling out exactly when and under what conditions you should enter and exit your swing trades.

The best way to explain the Master Plan rules is with an actual example, so we'll provide one. First, take a look at the standard candlestick chart shown in Figure 4.1, on the opposite page. It shows the recent price pattern of a stock that's clearly in a well-established long-term *uptrend* —i.e., it has a clearly bullish outlook. (The actual identity of the stock is irrelevant to our example; just take our word that it met the qualifying criteria outlined earlier.) However, as the four consecutive black candles show, it's recently experienced a short-term *pullback* (indicated by the arrow). Thus, as you now know, it is a prime candidate for a *long* swing trade.

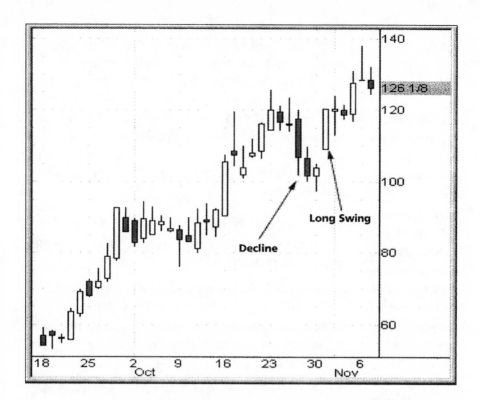

Long Swing

Decline

Entering the Trade

Swing-trading opportunities are *always* identified *after* the market closes, based on chart patterns that include that day's price performance. However, trades aren't entered until the morning of the following trading day — and then not until *several minutes after the market has opened*, by which time you have had a chance to evaluate the stock's initial price action. That action determines exactly when you enter your trade, as well as the decision rule you use in setting your desired entry price.

The key factor in every case is whether the stock opened the day's trading at a price near the previous

FIGURE 4.1
The chart above shows a classic pattern signaling a bullish swing trading entry opportunity.

day's closing level—or whether it "gapped" up or down from that prior closing price. According to the definition we use in the Master Plan, a stock is considered to have "gapped up" when it opens *higher* than the previous day's close *by 50 cents or more.* Likewise, it is considered to have "gapped down" any time it opens *50 cents or more below* the prior day's close. Most usually, however, a stock will open *within 50 cents* of its prior-day close, neither gapping up nor gapping down.

Based on these definitions, here are the Master Plan's recommended guidelines regarding *when* to enter your trade-opening orders:

- If the stock opens *within 50 cents (half a point) of its prior-day close*—the most common occurrence under normal market conditions—you should place your entry order *within a few minutes* after the market opens.

- Should the stock *gap up by 50 cents or more* from the prior day's close, you should *wait at least 30 minutes* after the market opens before placing your entry order. (**Note:** This condition applies only when opening a bullish trade—i.e., when buying the stock. Were you opening a *bearish* trade—i.e., *selling short*—you would wait 30 minutes after the market opened only if the stock's price *gapped down* 50 cents or more from the prior day's close.)

- Should the stock *gap down by 50 cents or more* from the previous day's close, you should place your entry order *approximately 5 minutes* after the market opens. (**Note:** Once again, this restriction applies only when opening a bullish trade—i.e., buying the stock. Were you opening a *bearish*

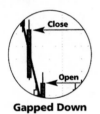

Gapped Down

trade, or *selling short*, you would enter your order *approximately 5 minutes* after the market opens only when the stock *gaps up by 50 cents or more* from the previous day's close.)

Setting the Entry Price for Your Swing Trade

As is the case with *when* to enter your trade, the *price* at which you initiate your swing-trade position depends on whether or not the stock has gapped up, or down, at the opening. Once again, under typical market conditions, stock prices do NOT gap higher or lower at the opening, but begin trading at or near the previous day's closing level. When that's what happens, the limit price you specify in your opening order should be based on prior-day prices. However, when the stock you're planning to buy (or sell short) DOES gap higher or lower, you should base the limit price you set in your opening order on the current day's prices (i.e., those at which the stock traded *after* the gap opening).

Based on those conditions, here are the Master Plan rules for setting the limit price specified in your opening swing-trade order:

When to enter your trade — the price at which you initiate your swing-trade position depends on whether or not the stock has gapped up, or down, at the opening.

- If the stock opens *within 50 cents (half a point) of its prior-day close* — once again, the most common occurrence under normal market conditions — you should *buy* the stock as soon as it trades at a level *6 cents (1/16th of a point) above* the previous day's high. This can be accomplished by using a "buy stop" order, and greatly increases the likelihood that the stock is moving in the direction of the primary bullish trend — i.e., rebounding from its most recent minor pullback. (**Note:** If you are attempting to enter a *bearish* trade — i.e., selling the stock short — you enter as soon as the stock trades at a level *6 cents below* the previous day's *low* price. This can be accomplished using a "sell stop" order, and again increases the likelihood the stock is moving in the direction of the primary bearish trend — i.e., pulling back from the peak of its most recent short-term rally.)

A **"buy stop"** is an order to purchase a stock should the share price rise (or fall) to a pre-specified level. It can be used to initiate a new long trade or close out a short position.

A **"sell stop"** is an order to sell a stock should the share price fall (or rise) to a pre-specified level. It can be used to sell shares you currently own or to initiate a new short position.

- Should the stock *gap up* OR *down by 50 cents or more* from the prior day's close, buy the stock as soon as it trades *6 cents above* the *current day's high*. This should be done *at least 30 minutes* after the stock *gaps up* at the opening, or *5 minutes* after the stock *gaps down* at the opening. Again, this can be accomplished using a "buy stop" order. (**Note:** For *bearish* trades, the price for the limit order to sell short should be set *6 cents below* the *current day's low*. The order should be placed *at least 30 minutes* after a *gap-down opening*, or *5 minutes* after a *gap-up opening*. A "sell stop" order will once again work to initiate this version of the trade.)

Immediately Get Ready to Exit

With long-term investments, once a position is opened, you typically give a sigh of thanks, then sit back and wait (sometimes for months, or even longer) for something good to happen. When you swing trade, however, that's definitely NOT the case. What you do instead is immediately position yourself to take a rapid profit — or to quickly bail out if prices turn against you — again based on specific rules provided in our Master Plan.

These rules, designed to encourage locking-in profits, and strictly limiting losses, in order to preserve your capital, are actually fairly conservative relative to similar guidelines for most other short-term trading strategies. They call for:

- **Setting an initial *profit target* of approximately *7 percent (7.0%)*.** In the case of *bullish* swing trades, in which you buy stock, this means setting a "limit-sell" order at a price roughly *7 percent above your entry point*. And, in the case of *bearish* swing trades involving the short sale of stock, it means setting a "limit-buy" order at a price about *7 percent below your entry price*.

- **Setting a rigid *stop loss* that limits your risk exposure to *a maximum of 4 percent (4.0%)*.** In *bullish* trades, this means immediately placing a "sell-stop" order — and, in *bearish* trades, it means quickly putting in a "buy-stop" order. The actual positioning of these stop orders is a bit complicated, so read the following explanation carefully.

In a *bullish* trade, the sell-stop is placed at a price *4 percent below your entry price*, or at a price *6 cents below the low* on the day that was used to set the entry price—whichever is *higher*. To clarify, if the stock you bought opened *without a gap* on the day of purchase, the stop would be placed at a price 6 *cents below the previous day's low*—if that price was *higher* than the stop price that would be set by the 4 percent rule. But, if the stock you bought opened *with a gap* on the day of purchase, then the stop would be placed at a price 6 *cents below the current day's low*—again assuming that price was *higher* than the stop price set by the 4 percent rule.

In *bearish* trades, the opposite would apply. Specifically, you would place the buy stop at a level *4 percent above your entry price*, or at a price 6 *cents above the high* on the day that was used to set the entry price—whichever is *lower*. Clarifying once again, if the stock you sold short opened *without a gap* on the day of purchase, the buy stop would be placed at a price 6 *cents above the previous day's high*—if that price was *lower* than the stop price that would be set by the 4 percent rule. However, if the stock you sold short opened *with a gap* on the day of purchase, then the stop would be positioned at a price 6 *cents above the current day's high*—again assuming that price was *lower* than the stop price set by the 4 percent rule.

These stop-loss rules seem complex at first glance, and we'll admit they are a bit complicated. However, you'll get the hang of how they work fairly quickly once you start using them regularly. Besides, in all likelihood, you'll never have to actually figure them yourself. With the sophisticated account-management software provided by most online brokerages these days, you can simply enter your desired stop-loss criteria and, if you check a specific box, the program will automatically calculate the desired stop price and place the appropriate stop orders for you. You can even have the program recalculate stop levels and adjust the orders to reflect price action on subsequent days — which brings us to the next refinement of our Master Plan rules.

What to Do the Day *After* You Open Your Trade

As already noted, the primary goal of the swing-trading Master Plan is to increase your profits and strictly control your losses so as to promote steady growth of your capital base. Doing this, however, requires diligently monitoring your positions each day they're open, and adjusting your stop orders based on that day's price action. It also requires taking your profits according to a predetermined plan whenever your targets are reached.

Following are the Master Plan rules for managing your open positions on a day-to-day basis — and for closing them at the optimum time — beginning with the guidelines for steadily reducing (or perhaps even eliminating) your chances of suffering a loss. This latter process is known as using a "trailing stop loss."

Once your trade execution is confirmed and you know your opening price, the first thing you do is set your initial stop-loss level and enter the corresponding order. The next action you take comes shortly after the opening the following day. At that point, as you did when you were preparing to initiate your trade in the first place, you closely watch the opening action of your stock. If it opens at a price near the previous day's

A trailing stop loss is the process of steadily reducing — or perhaps even eliminating — your chances of suffering a loss by progressively raising your stop level as a stock's price rises (in a long position), or lowering it as the price falls (in a short position).

close — i.e., if it *doesn't* gap up or down by 50 cents or more — you adjust your stop-loss level based on the prior-day prices. However, if it *does* gap up or down by 50 cents or more per share, you change the stop-loss level based on the current day's prices.

In either case, the rules for repositioning the stop are the same, as follows:

A normal opening.

- For *long positions* in a stock that has *a normal (non-gap) opening*, calculate whether a stop price *6 cents below* the previous day's *low* would be *higher* than your existing stop price. If it would, *raise* your stop-loss level to this new price and adjust your limit order accordingly.

- For *long positions* in a stock that *does have a gap opening*, wait *30 minutes for a gap down* or *5 minutes for a gap up*, then *raise* your stop-loss level if a stop *6 cents below* today's low would be *higher* than your existing stop price. Again, adjust your limit order accordingly.

A gap opening.

- For *short positions* in a stock that has *a normal (non-gap) opening*, calculate whether a stop price *6 cents above* the previous day's *high* would be *lower* than your existing stop price. If it would, *lower* your stop-loss level to this new price and adjust your limit order accordingly.

- For *short positions* in a stock that *does have a gap opening*, wait *30 minutes for a gap up* or *5 minutes for a gap down*, then *lower* your stop-loss level if a stop *6 cents above* today's *high* would be *lower* than your existing stop price. Again, adjust your limit order accordingly.

Enhancing Your Profit Prospects

Now for the refinements in the Master Plan rules designed to enhance your profit prospects. When you place the order establishing your initial profit target, you apply it to *only half* of the shares you purchase (or sell short, in the case of bearish trades). Once your target is reached and your closing order is executed, locking in a gain of 7 percent on half your stock, you *hold the remaining half* of your shares to benefit from any further price increase. Your hope is that you'll be able to "ride the full wave" on this particular short-term swing, thereby maximizing your overall profit.

However, you don't want to have too much of your existing profit riding on that hope, so you immediately enter a stop order to exit the rest of the position. This stop order is positioned in exactly the same fashion as described above for your original trailing stop-loss orders. (In fact, it becomes the *only* stop in force for the remaining half of your now-profitable position.) To be precise:

- For a *long position*, your shares are sold when the price drops to a level 6 *cents below* the *prior day's low* (if there was *no gap opening*), or 6 *cents below* the *current day's low* (if there was *a gap opening*).

- For a *short position*, your shares are repurchased when the price rises to a level 6 *cents above* the *prior day's high* (if there was *no gap opening*), *or 6 cents above* the *current day's high* (if there was *a gap opening*).

It *Is* Complex—But It Works

FIGURE 4.2
Flow Chart
showing all
possible trading
actions for a
bullish "long
swing" trade.

Figure 4.2, shown below, features a flow chart that shows all the possible actions for a bullish (long) swing trade. That should help clarify the above instructions—which, as we noted earlier, *ARE* fairly complex. However, it is well worth learning and following them, simply because *they work*.

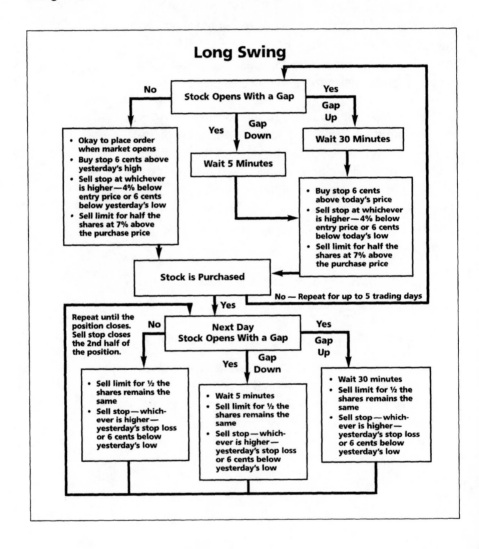

In even the worst case, the maximum possible loss on a single trade is 4 percent, which virtually ensures you'll be able to preserve enough capital to participate in future trades. Plus, because of the diligent use of trailing stop-loss orders, it's probable that your typical loss will be much less than 4 percent. Likewise, the exit strategy for profitable trades makes it highly likely that your typical profit will exceed the 7 percent level you set as your initial target. In addition, because of the trend-following nature of swing trading, you'll typically have a far larger number of winning trades than losing trades, compounding the initial 7%-4% profit-loss advantage.

Remember, however, that the success or failure of your swing trades is not entirely dependent on the performance of the individual stocks you buy or sell short. The movement of the entire market is very, very powerful. Thus, when the market is moving with your trades, a very high percentage of them — even those involving weaker issues — will prove profitable. However, when the entire market begins moving against your positions, a higher-than-expected percentage of them will produce losses. Fortunately, if you rigorously adhere to our stop-loss guidelines, those losses should never become excessive.

A Bit More Information on Short Swing Trades

Because most of the actions discussed so far have been keyed to long swing trades (bullish positions), with bearish alternatives explained primarily in terms of "opposites," we want to take a minute and provide just a bit more information regarding short swing trades.

Because of the diligent use of trailing stop-loss orders, it's probable that your typical loss will be much less than 4 percent. Likewise, the exit strategy for profitable trades makes it highly likely that your typical profit will exceed the 7 percent level you set as your initial target.

Obviously, you use a short swing trade to make money when you feel a stock has a bearish outlook — i.e., when it is moving in an established downward trend that is expected to continue. To initiate a short swing trade, you do what is referred to as "selling the stock short." This essentially means that you sell the stock without ever having owned it, hoping to buy the shares back later at a lower price and pocket the price difference as profit. (Technically, your broker "borrows" the stock from another client and loans it to you so you can sell it. When you later "cover" your position by buying the stock back, you return it to the broker, who credits it back to the account from which it was borrowed.)

With a couple of minor differences, a short swing trade is a mirror reflection of a bullish (or long) trade, and the rationale behind it is the same. To wit, stocks in a primary downtrend tend to have periodic short-term rallies that interrupt the downward price progression. Your goal in initiating a short swing is to sell the stock short at the top, or peak, of one of these rallies and then ride the position back to the lower limit of the stock's downward-sloping trading range. At that point, you take your profits by covering the short position (i.e., buying the stock back). A candlestick chart showing a stock in a downtrend that is conducive to short swing trading is featured in Figure 4.3, on the opposite page.

Notice in the chart that the downtrend is interrupted by several short-term rallies. The arrows indicate placement of short swing trades, opened near the peak of these rallies, but *after* the stock had resumed its downtrend. These entries were signaled when the price fell below the low price of the previous trading day. Refer back to the Master Plan description for details on the

To initiate a short swing trade, you do what is referred to as "selling the stock short." This essentially means that you sell the stock without ever having owned it, hoping to buy the shares back later at a lower price and pocket the price difference as profit.

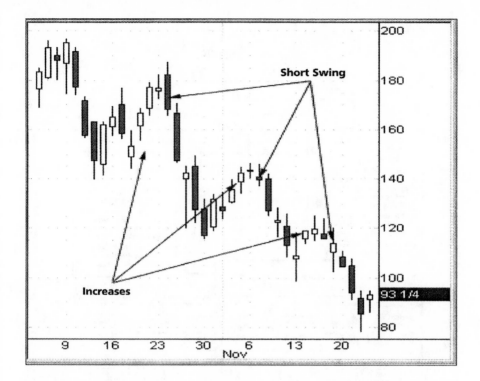

rules for opening bearish swing trades—or refer to the schematic diagram featured in Figure 4.4, on the following page. It provides instructions for how to adjust the stop-loss levels on trading days subsequent to the short sale of the stock, as well as guidelines on how to exit at both a profit and a loss.

A Final Word on the Master Plan

You've now been introduced to the basic fundamentals of swing trading, as well as the entry and exit rules, risk-control methods and other guidelines featured in our Master Plan. When you finish the remainder of this book and begin doing additional research into the resources available to help you get actually

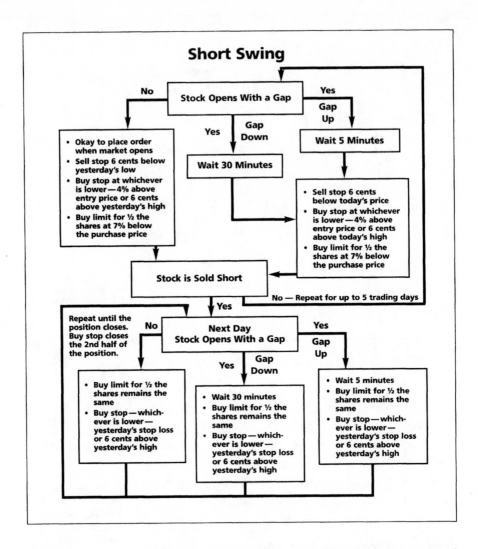

Short Swing

Stock Opens With a Gap

- No → Okay to place order when market opens
  - Sell stop 6 cents below yesterday's low
  - Buy stop at whichever is lower—4% above entry price or 6 cents above yesterday's high
  - Buy limit for ½ the shares at 7% below the purchase price

- Yes / Gap Down → Wait 30 Minutes

- Yes / Gap Up → Wait 5 Minutes
  - Sell stop 6 cents below today's price
  - Buy stop at whichever is lower—4% above entry price or 6 cents above today's high
  - Buy limit for ½ the shares at 7% below the purchase price

Stock is Sold Short

No — Repeat for up to 5 trading days

Yes

Next Day Stock Opens With a Gap

- No → Repeat until the position closes. Buy stop closes the 2nd half of the position.
  - Buy limit for ½ the shares remains the same
  - Buy stop—whichever is lower—yesterday's stop loss or 6 cents above yesterday's high

- Yes / Gap Down → Wait 30 minutes
  - Buy limit for ½ the shares remains the same
  - Buy stop—whichever is lower—yesterday's stop loss or 6 cents above yesterday's high

- Yes / Gap Up → Wait 5 minutes
  - Buy limit for ½ the shares remains the same
  - Buy stop—whichever is lower—yesterday's stop loss or 6 cents above yesterday's high

FIGURE 4.4 Flow Chart showing all possible bearish "short swing" trading actions.

involved in swing trading, you'll no doubt be exposed to a number of different software programs, advisory services and interactive brokerage firm websites. Many feature advanced analytical tools, use complex technical indicators and provide entry and exit signals based on complex algorithms and other mysterious mathematical formulae.

There's little doubt these tools of the analytical wizard's art can provide valuable insight into such areas as trend development and continuation. However, they can also unnecessarily complicate your efforts to achieve swing-trading success.

By contrast, the rules and guidelines provided in our Master Plan — which, in truth, were developed using many of the same indicators and formulae just mentioned — are relatively concise, clear and easy to implement. And, they have a proven record of success.

So, why not rely on them to get you started — resisting the inclination too many novices have to make swing trading a lot harder than it needs to be. Then, move on to more complicated applications as you get more experience under your belt.

CHAPTER 5

Some Swing-Trading Case Studies

In Chapter 2, we provided an overview of the basic elements involved in technical analysis, which is used to analyze market price and volume data, as well as produce the various types of charts that can be used to illustrate trends, and thereby generate swing-trading entry signals. While looking at charts is a good way to find appropriate candidates for swing trading, it can also be very time consuming — especially if you do it every day. For that reason, we recommend that you find and use a good software package that can screen stocks based on a variety of technical indicators and provide a list of those with promising chart patterns. This process, known as "pattern recognition," can combine the review of simple descriptive variables, such as high and low prices and average volume over a specific period, with analysis of more advanced indicators, ranging from simple moving averages to complex oscillators.

While it's not necessary to have an in-depth understanding of these indicators in order to be a successful swing trader, it is helpful to have a basic knowledge of some of the more widely used pattern recog-

We recommend that you find and use a good software package that can screen stocks based on a variety of technical indicators and provide a list of those with promising chart patterns.

nition criteria, as well as an idea of how they look when presented in chart form, and the impact they can have on your trading decisions (whether you make them or they're generated by an automated software package, or advisory service). To that end, we'll briefly describe some of our favorite indicators, then look at some examples of how they appear on candlestick and Equivolume charts. We'll then wrap up with several swin- trading case studies, presenting illustrations that show a trade-triggering chart pattern and list the criteria that prompted both entry to, and exit from, that particular trade.

Favorite Indicators Used to Recognize Swing-Trading Patterns

Four indicators we do want to take a closer look at include:

- **moving averages (MA)**
- **"Force Index"**
- **directional movement index (DMI)**
- **"Up/Down/In/Out" overlay**

In laying the groundwork for presentation of our Master Plan, we've already discussed some of our more basic trade-selection criteria, such as the insistence that eligible stocks have a price of at least $12 and an average daily trading volume of 500,000 shares, or more. These are more important for their "protective" qualities than their analytical value—i.e., market makers can't manipulate such stocks as easily as they can low-price, low-volume issues—so we won't devote any more time to them than we already have.

However, four indicators we do want to take a closer look at include moving averages (MA), the so-called "Force Index," the directional movement index (DMI) and the "Up/Down/In/Out" overlay—a proprietary indicator available only on the recently updated **Swing-Tracker** software program. Let's start with a discussion of moving averages.

A Look at Moving Averages

A moving average is simply the average closing price of a stock or index calculated over a specific number of days, usually ranging from 10 to 200. It's called a "moving" average because, on each new day, the current day's closing price is added to the average, while the oldest day's price is dropped. The average is then recalculated, based on this formula:

Simple MA = (P1 + P2 + ... + Pn) / n
where "P" is the price being averaged
and "n" is the number of days in the average

In addition to the *simple* (or *arithmetic*) moving average (SMA) calculated by the above formula, there are four other popular types of moving averages: *exponential, triangular, variable* and *weighted*. Moving averages can also be calculated based on a number of indicators other than the closing price, including opening, high and low prices, as well as volume.

As the security's price changes, its average price moves up or down. All moving averages smooth the pattern of a stock's price movement—the more days in the moving average, the smoother the resulting pattern line—making it easier to identify trends. It is also significant to know where the current price is, relative to the position of the various moving averages, as well as whether the shorter-time-frame moving averages are above, or below, the longer-time-frame MA's. For this purpose, we typically focus on just three moving averages—those covering 10 days, 20 days and 50 days.

Working only with the 10- and 20-day simple moving averages (SMA), we can identify two distinct indica-

A moving average is simply the average closing price of a stock or index calculated over a specific number of days, usually ranging from 10 to 200.

tors that a given stock is in an uptrend and might thus be suitable for a long swing trade. These are:

- Today's closing price is above both the 10-day and 20-day moving averages.
- The 10-day moving average is above the 20-day moving average.

Trends have a number of identifying characteristics that can be linked to analysis of moving averages.

For an uptrend, these include:

Uptrend

- A pattern of *higher* highs and *higher* lows.
- *Rising* 10- and 20-day MA's.
- Higher volume on the *upward* legs.
- Closing prices *above* the 20- and 50-day MA's.
- An uptrend stock will find *support* at either the 20- or 50-day MA.

For a downtrend, the identifying characteristics include:

Downtrend

- A pattern of *lower* highs and *lower* lows.
- *Falling* 10- and 20-day MA's.
- Higher volume on the *downward* legs.
- Closing prices *below* the 20- and 50-day MA's.
- A downtrend stock will find *resistance* at either the 20- or 50-day MA.

The chart for the NASDAQ 100 Index, shown in Figure 5.1, on the opposite page, illustrates how the 10-, 20- and 50-day moving averages are depicted graphically. It also shows the display of the "Force Index," which we'll discuss next.

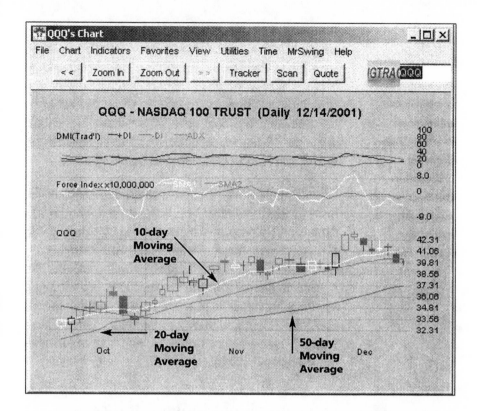

FIGURE 5.1
This chart of
the NASDAQ 100
Index illustrates
how 10-, 20-
and 50-day
moving averages
are depicted
graphically.

Dr. Elder's 'Force Index' — A New Way of Using Volume

Next, let's look at the so-called "Force Index," an oscillator developed by Dr. Alexander Elder and detailed in his book, *Trading for a Living*. The Force Index combines the three most essential pieces of market information — the direction of price change, its extent and trading volume. It provides a new, practical way of using volume to make trading decisions, and is calculated using this formula:

Force Index = Volume (today)
x [Close (today) - Close (yesterday)]

Although the Force Index can be used raw, we prefer to smooth it with moving averages—specifically those covering 3 days (FI-3MA) and 13 days (FI-13MA). A 3-day moving average of the Force Index is a very sensitive indicator showing the short-term battle between the bulls and the bears over a given stock or index, while the 13-day Force Index MA identifies the longer-term battle between bullish and bearish traders.

When the FI-13MA is greater than zero and the FI-3MA is less than zero, the bulls are winning, which signals an uptrend and a potential opportunity to do a long swing trade. And, when the situation is reversed—i.e., the FI-13MA is less than zero and the FI-3MA is greater than zero—the bears are winning, meaning the stock is in a downtrend and conditions could be ripe for a short swing trade. Once again, Figure 5.1, above, illustrates how the Force Index moving averages are displayed on an Equivolume chart.

The Directional Moving Index— A Trend-Following Indicator

The "Directional Movement Index" (DMI) is a trend-following indicator developed by J. Welles Wilder, Jr. It was designed to help traders determine whether a stock or index is in a trending or non-trending market. Since the market is in a strong trend only about 30 percent of the time, and moving sideways the remaining 70 percent of the time, this indicator can be used to identify periods in which the market is showing significant trending or directional behavior.

The actual calculation of the DMI is fairly complex, so we won't bother with the math or the equations involved. Instead, we'll just describe how it's displayed on charts, and how to quickly interpret it. Essentially, the display of the DMI consists of three lines:

+DI—The current positive directional index, which is the range of highs divided by the price range over the last day (including the prior day's close), smoothed over a given number of periods.

-DI—The current negative directional index, which is the range of lows divided by the price range over the last day (including the prior day's close), smoothed over a given number of periods.

ADX—A modified moving average of the difference between +DI and -DI, divided by the sum of +DI and -DI, multiplied by 100.

FIGURE 5.2
The top panel of this chart for Olin Corp. shows the three DMI indicators as they are depicted in most charting software programs.

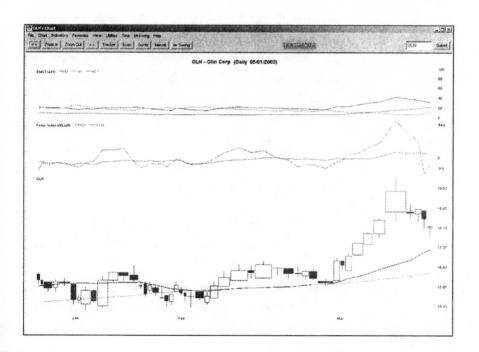

The DMI signals an uptrend when the ADX is greater than 30 (the higher the better), and the +DI line is higher than the –DI line. Conversely, the DMI signals a downtrend when the ADX is greater than 30 (again, the higher the better), and the –DI line is higher than the +DI line. The chart for Olin Corp. (OLN), shown in Figure 5.2 on the previous page, illustrates how the DMI appears on an Equivolume price chart.

Introducing the Up/Down/In/Out Indicator

Up/Down/In/Out is a chart overlay available only in mrswing.com's proprietary SwingTracker software program. However, it is a valuable indicator, so we felt you should at least be familiar with it if you plan to be an active swing trader.

What Up/Down/In/Out does is color-code the individual bars, or candlesticks, on charts, based on price movement in order to illustrate the relationship between the current high and low price and the previous day's high and low price. Here's an explanation of what the four elements of the overlay indicate:

- **Up (green)** indicates that the current *high* is *higher* than the previous high and the current *low* is *higher* than the previous low.

- **Down (red)** indicates the current *high* is *lower* than the previous high and the current *low* is *lower* than the previous low.

- **In (yellow)** indicates the current *high* is *lower* than the previous high, and the current *low* is *higher* than previous low.

- **Out (blue)** indicates that the current *high* is *high-er* than the previous high, and the current *low* is *lower* than the previous low.

Because this book isn't being printed in color, we can't illustrate exactly how much the overlay enhances your ability to interpret chart price relationships, which is an important element in setting your swing-trade stops as spelled out in the Master Plan rules. However, if you visit the mrswing.com website, you'll be able to see several examples of how this indicator actually appears.

On to the Case Studies

You've now been introduced to a few more of our favorite indicators and seen a couple of examples of how they appear on Equivolume-style candlestick charts. Now take a look at Figures 5.3, 5.4, 5.5 and Figure 5.6, which follow, just to get some additional impressions of how the various indicators appear on charts and thereby increase your understanding of how to interpret them.

Then, once you've done that, review Figures 5.7, 5.8 and 5.9. The charts in those illustrations depict actual conditions when successful swing trades were initiated, and the text under each of the charts detail the indicators that led to the opening of the trades, the actual prices that were used, what led to the trades being closed and the final profit on each position. With that experience under your belt — and the information you've gleaned from reading the rest of this book — you should be fully prepared to begin your own quest for potentially profitable swing-trading opportunities.

Figure 5.3
This illustration shows the price movements of Georgia Pacific Corp. (GP) as depicted in an Equivolume chart. Review it, as well as those on the following two pages, not for any specific signal, but rather to get a feel for how the various indicators just discussed appear on Equivolume charts.

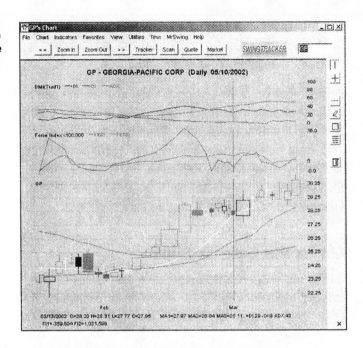

FIGURE 5.4
A sample Equivolume chart for KT Corporation (KTC)

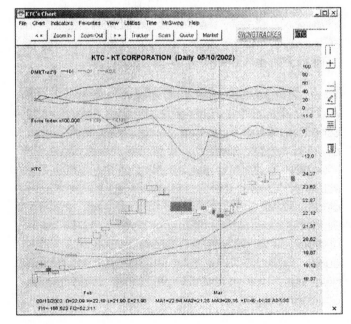

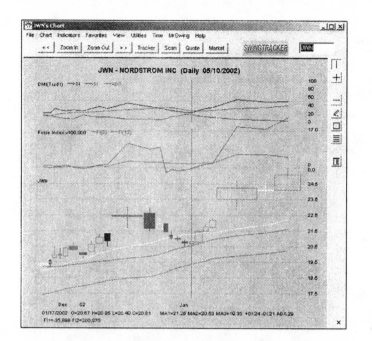

FIGURE 5.5
A sample
Equivolume
chart for
Nordstrom,
Inc. (JWN)

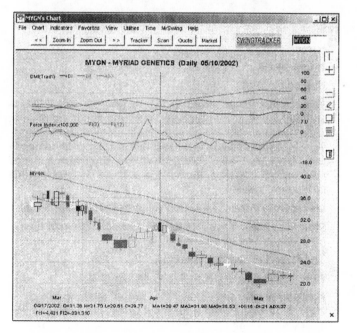

FIGURE 5.6
A sample
Equivolume
chart for
Myriad
Genetics
(MYGN)

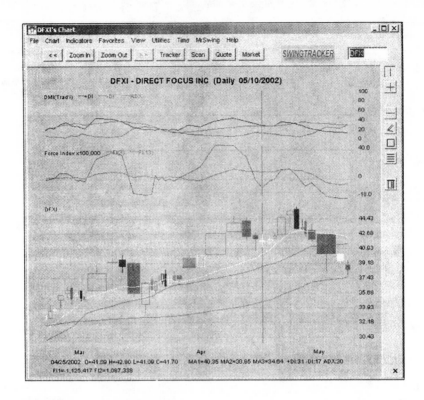

Figure 5.7   **Trade: DFXI**

Date: 04/26/2002

Reasons for trade/setup: CLOSE > SMAC50 and CLOSE > SMAC20 (to be sure the stock is still in an uptrend) and HIGH < HIGH1 and HIGH1 < HIGH2 AND (the stock must be experiencing a 3-day decline/pullback within the context of an uptrend) and FORCE3<=0 AND FORCE13>=0 (the short-term battle is now won by the bears, but still the bulls are in control of the longer-term battle)

Swing Entry Price: $42.48 (High of yesterday $42.42 + $0.06)

Stop Loss Price: $41.35 (order $0.06 below the low of the previous day $41.41 - $0.06)

Target: $45.45 (entry price +7%)

Exit: $45.45 (05/02/2002) & $43.44 (05/02/2002)

Reason for exit: $45.45 at a **7%** gain on the **long** swing trade & $43.44 trailing stop low of yesterday $43.50 - $0.06

Profit/loss: $1.965 = ($2.97 + $0.96)/2 or gain of 4.63%

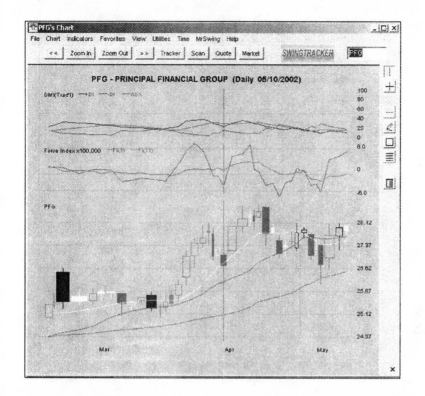

Trade: PFG   **FIGURE 5.8**

Date: 04/12/2002

Reasons for trade/setup: CLOSE > SMAC50 and CLOSE > SMAC20 (to be sure the stock is still in an uptrend) and HIGH < HIGH1 and HIGH1 < HIGH2 AND (the stock must be experiencing a 3-day decline/pullback within the context of an uptrend) and FORCE3<=0 AND FORCE13>=0 (the short-term battle is now won by the bears, but still the bulls are in control of the longer-term battle)

Swing Entry price: $27.26 (High of yesterday $27.20 + $0.06)

Stop Loss price: $26.35 (order $0.06 below the low of the previous day $26.41 - $0.06)

Target: $29.17 (entry price +7%)

Exit: $27.94 (04/18/2002)

Reason for exit: $27.94 trailing stop low of yesterday $28.00 - $0.06 & Target of 7% never met

Profit/loss: $0.68 or gain of 2.49%

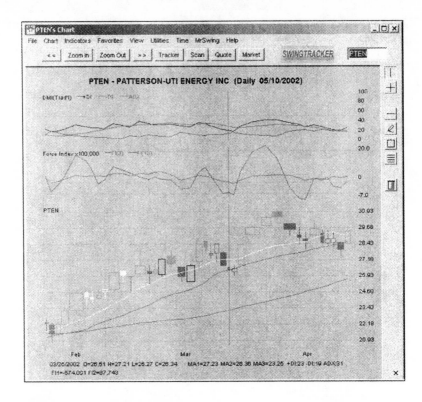

FIGURE 5.9 **Trade:** PTEN

Date: 03/26/2002

Reasons for trade/setup: CLOSE > SMAC50 and CLOSE > SMAC20 (to be sure the stock is still in an uptrend) and HIGH < HIGH1 and HIGH1 < HIGH2 AND (the stock must be experiencing a 3-day decline/pullback within the context of an uptrend) and FORCE3<=0 AND FORCE13>=0 (the short-term battle is now won by the bears, but still the bulls are in control of the longer-term battle)

Swing Entry price: $26.84 (High of yesterday $26.78 + $0.06)

Stop Loss price: $25.94 (order $0.06 below the low of the previous day $26.00 - $0.06)

Target: $28.72 (entry price +7%)

Exit: $28.72 (03/28/2002) & $29.99 (04/03/2002) at open

Reason for exit: $28.72 at a 7% gain on the long swing trade & $29.99 trailing stop low of yesterday $30.31 - $0.06

Profit/loss: $2.515 = ($1.88 + $3.15)/2 or gain of 9.37%

SUMMARY

The Up-and-Down
Path to Profits

You've now had a thorough introduction to swing trading — a "hybrid" investment methodology that eliminates many of the most nerve-wracking and frustrating features of both buy-and-hold investing and day trading, while minimizing risk and retaining a generous potential for profit. You've also learned the basic elements of technical analysis, reviewed how some of the key technical indicators are used, and seen how those indicators can be transformed into patterns on various types of charts. Plus, you've discovered how to use those charts as a means to recognize primary market trends and identify the best times to initiate new swing-trade positions. Finally, you've been given a proven set of rules and guidelines — our so-called Master Plan — which you can follow in determining when and how to both limit losses, and take profits, on your personal swing trades.

Obviously, this is a lot of information to absorb, and it may take some time — and some real-world experience — before you fully grasp all the finer points and subtle nuances of the swing-trading art.

Obviously, this is a lot of information to absorb, and it may take some time — *and some real-world experience* — before you fully grasp all the finer points and subtle nuances of the swing-trading art. Even without a thorough understanding of those details, however, you should have more than enough knowledge to be a successful swing trader. And, as you do more research on the subject — comparing brokerage firms, advisory service websites, software packages and other analytical tools — your level of knowledge will steadily increase, raising your measure of success right along with it.

After all, the driving principle of the swing concept is that you deal only in stocks which are already moving in an established trend — and you open only those positions, either long or short, that will profit from a continuation of that primary trend. And, as you've no doubt often heard, investment lore strongly contends that, "The trend is your friend." Thus, whether experienced pro or swing novice, *you'll have strong market forces on your side* in every trade you do.

You'll also have a clear-cut set of operating rules to ensure your losses will be minimized when you do turn out to be wrong. And make no mistake, no matter how much knowledge you acquire, or how much experience you garner, *you WILL still have losing trades*. That is the lone absolute with any investment strategy — swing trading not excluded.

Earning your success will also require you to put in more than a little effort — i.e., though it's fairly simple, swing trading is *NOT* a lazy man's way to riches. You'll have to work hard to identify good swing trading candidates and determine the optimum entry prices for your trades, as well as diligently monitor your positions every day to ensure you exit at the right time — and at the right price.

But, if you do all those things — exercising both patience and discipline — you will almost certainly roll up

The driving principle of the swing concept is that you deal only in stocks which are already moving in an established trend — and you open only those positions, either long or short, that will profit from a continuation of that primary trend.

far more winning trades than losers. And, ultimately, that means you should score *substantial overall gains* as a swing trader—something neither long-term investors nor day traders have been able to say with assurance in recent years.

So, without further delay, take what you've learned in this book—and *begin marching along the up-and-down path to swing trading profits.*

Key Resources for Swing Traders

I f you hope to be a truly successful swing trader, you'll need more resources at your disposal than just a pencil, a calculator and a few stock charts downloaded from a generic Internet financial news source. At a bare minimum, you will want some decent technical analysis charting software that's compatible with an online service that updates current market data and generates new charts based on the most recent prices. Obviously, there are any number of suitable software packages on the market, as well as numerous qualified data-service providers and analytical advisory services, and a handful that offer a complete line of both online and at-home analytical tools designed specifically for swing traders. Brief descriptions of the key services and packages are provided below, and we recommend that you at least check them out before deciding on which resources to use.

MrSwing.com is the website that provides access, either directly or via links, to all of the tools and services described below, as well as educational articles, products and an online store that sells charting software, analytical programs, books and other market-related items.

• **MrSwing Lite** is a free online newsletter on swing trading, which you can receive weekly by filling out a simple subscription form. The newsletter, in HTML format, features articles on trading strategy, product and book reviews, market commentary, educational information about swing trading and technical analysis, recaps of suggested trading rules, and recommendations on specific swing-trading opportunities, including advice on where to position your entry and exit orders, and how and at what price to take profits.

- **SwingTracker 4.0** is a software package designed specifically for swing and day traders. It features the necessary hook-up for direct access to current quotes; real-time Intra-day charting capacity, and screens that allow you to scan a given universe of stocks for trading opportunities, based on a wide variety of criteria, including more than two-dozen key technical indicators. Other special features include: Automatic application of Equivolume and Force Index indicators on charts, if desired; pre-designed stock scans you can use if you don't want to specify your own criteria and real-time alerts to swing-trading opportunities. Figure A.1, below, illustrates the kinds of real-time charts SwingTracker produces in response to real-time stock scans.

FIGURE A.1   **Illustration of SwingTracker Scan Screen**
Featuring chart and pricing info for Lockheed Martin

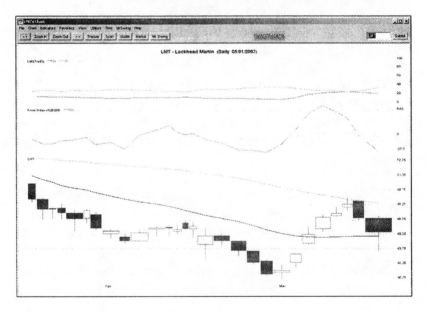

- **SwingLab** is a free online analytical service that works either independently or in conjunction with SwingTracker. It shows you many of the mathematical formulae used by **mrswing.com** in building specialized stock scans, and demonstrates how to use them. There are also step-by-step descriptions of how to set up the screens for running your own scans. SwingLab is updated regularly, so you should check it often for new information and trading advice.

- **MasterSwings** is **mrswing.com's** paid daily e-mail advisory service. Each day, subscribers receive Swing-Trading Alerts identifying the most promising long and short trades of the day. Alerts are generated by **mrswing.com's** state-of-the-art swing-trading models, which scan a universe of 9,000-plus stocks, utilizing a variety of technical indicators and select only those potential trades that offer an optimum chance for profit with a strictly limited risk. Each day's e-mail advisory features four different trade categories (bullish, bearish, reversals, and breakout-breakdown swings), with four different trade recommendations in each category. The alerts also feature entry, exit and money-management specifics for each recommended trade.

Interactive Brokers and optionsXpress

Now, a more detailed look at two of the discount online brokers we prefer — just so you can see the features they have that are of particular value to swing traders.

Interactive Brokers

Interactive Brokers is a discount firm that's ideal for swing trading. It offers an order feature called **one cancels all (OCA)**. This feature allows you to enter the three components of an order as a group. For example, for a **long swing** trade, this would include:

- A **buy stop** to buy the stock when the price moves above the stop price.
- A **sell stop** to sell the shares if the price moves **down 4%**.
- A **sell limit** to lock in profits (on half the shares) when the price **rises 7%**.

In other words, you are able to enter sell orders even before the stock is purchased. They then become active once the purchase transaction is completed. If only part of the **buy order** is filled (for example, half the shares), the quantity of the **sell orders** is adjusted accordingly. Once the stock is purchased, if either of the **sell orders** is executed, the other is **automatically canceled**. The OCA option is fairly rare among online brokers — but very valuable.

Using these features, you can place your orders before the market opens and forget about them until the evening or the next day. You're probably saying, "But what if the market gaps up or down? The rules are different?" That's true, but gap openings happen infrequently — and you can often predict if a stock is likely to gap up or down by checking the prices in **after-hours trading**. If you have a concern, simply wait — but, if you're relatively sure a stock is likely to open within 50 cents of the prior-day close, go ahead and place orders for that position.

Interactive brokers also offers other features valuable to both swing traders and other types of investors. These include:

- Streaming real-time quotes, including after-hours prices.
- High-speed execution.
- Very low commissions — 1 cent ($0.01) a share, with a minimum of $1.00.
- Execution in stocks, options, futures and options on futures.
- Execution of trades on 40 exchanges in 16 countries.
- Multi-currency trading for international clients.

For further details, or to see about opening an account for your own swing trades, go to **www.interactivebrokers.com**.

optionsXpress

optionsXpress is another discount brokerage firm we like because of its many features favorable to swing traders. While the name suggests a specialist in options, you can trade stocks, bonds and mutual funds as well. optionsXpress also has a unique autotrading service called **Xecute™** that **mrswing.com** uses for several of its services. Their daily swing-trading recommendations also go directly to optionsXpress, which will automatically place the buy and sell orders for your account. This is a particularly convenient feature for subscribers who are unable to watch the market.

For swing traders, optionsXpress has a feature called **one cancels other (OCO)**. Once a long trade is placed, both closing sell orders (the limit and the stop) can be placed simultaneously. Then, when one is executed, the other will automatically be canceled. optionsXpress is also working on a feature (which will likely be ready by the time you read this) that will allow buy and sell orders to be placed simultaneously – a sign of their commitment to make improvements based on the needs of their swing-trading customers.

optionsXpress also offers other features valuable to both swing traders and other types of investors. These include:

- Streaming real-time quotes, including after-hours prices
- High-speed execution
- Low commissions – e.g., $19.95, $14.95 for mutual funds and up to 10 option contracts
- State-of-the-art charting, technical analysis and order-entry features in their account-management software
- Up-to-the-minute commentary and broad-market statistics
- Features specifically designed for options traders, such as the ability to easily trade both puts and calls, and to place orders for such combinations as spreads, straddles, strangles and butterflies
- Tools especially designed for options traders, including **Option Dragon** (a screening tool) and **Option Pricer**
- Option-trading approval for retirement and custodial accounts

For further details, or to see about opening an account for your own swing trades, go to **www.optionsxpress.com**

Resource Guide
Tools for Success in Trading

Recommended Reading

Advanced Swing Trading

By John Crane

Swing trading, a powerful technical approach for profiting from shorter-term price moves (several days to a couple of months) - is sweeping the trading world. And once you've mastered the basics, you're ready to tackle the innovative and accurate swing-trading system outlined in John Crane's new bestseller.

$69.95. Item #T190X-1199048

Tools and Tactics for the Master Day Trader

By Oliver Velez and Greg Capra

A no-nonsense, straight-shooting guide from the founder of Pristine.com, designed for active, self-directed traders. Provides potent trading strategies, technical skills, intuitive insights on discipline, psychology and winning methods for capturing more winning trades, more often.

$55.00. Item #T190X-11221

▲ ▲ ▲ ▲ ▲ ▲

These books along with thousands of others are available at a discount from Traders' Library. To place an order or to find out more, **call 1-800-272-2855** *or visit our web site at*

www.traderslibrary.com

Swing Trading
Power Strategies to Cut Risk and Boost Profits

By Jon Markman

Ideal for today's active traders, swing-trading bridges the gap between long-term "buy-&-holders" and day traders. Now, CNBC/MSN Money's Jon Markman presents the highly profitable, risk-abating benefits of swing trading in a thorough, move-by-move playbook for swing trading in the big leagues.

$29.95. Item #T190X-821613

The Master Swing Trader
Tools and Techniques to Profit from Outstanding Short-Term Trading Opportunities

By Alan Farley

Enter the hidden world of master pattern recognition and build powerful swing-trading strategies that respond quickly to changing market conditions. This complete, practical guide to modern swing trading includes over 180 illustrations and dozens of proprietary setups that illustrate both classic and highly original short-term tactics.

$55.00. Item #T190X-11668

Market Evaluation and Analysis for Swing Trading

By David S. Nassar and Bill Lupien

Nassar and Lupien, two of the industry's most influential traders, share with readers their techniques and strategies for successful swing trading in today's market. You'll learn how to work the market to your advantage by recognizing supply and demand imbalances, reading the strength of bids and offers, and spotting market maker trading patterns. This "must-have" guide is an essential resource for every swing trader.

$55.00. Item #T190X-1661626

Beginner's Guide to Short-Term Trading

By Toni Turner

Toni Turner does it again! This bestselling author and trading coach, delivers another strategy-packed guide for short-term trading. Ideal for anyone new to the game — and those looking for ways to boost their short-term trading profits — it's compact, to-the-point and filled with need-to-know facts.

$15.95.   Item #T190X-41613

The Candlestick Course

By Steve Nison

Get instruction from the expert in Candlestick Charting, Steve Nison. In this easy-to-understand book, Nison explains the practical applications of this hot new trend. By providing quizzes, Q&As, and intensive examples, Nison gives readers the knowledge they need to get involved in this new financial concept.

$59.95.   Item #T190X-84668

The New Market Wizards
Conversations With America's Top Traders

By Jack Schwager

In the classic hard-cover version, this title is a true investment "Bible." In-depth interviews with key players expose every facet of their winning strategies for consistently outperforming peers. See how you can do it, too!

$39.95.   Item #T190X-2106

Call **1-800-272-2855** *or visit our web site at*

www.traderslibrary.com

Encyclopedia of Chart Patterns

By Thomas Bulkowski

In addition to utilizing various indicators that help identify trends, there is a multitude of chart patterns in this new book that will tell the analyst whether the stock or commodity is in a bullish or bearish mode. Also included in this book are patterns that tell the analyst what the stock is going to do, based on where its price has been.

$79.95. Item #T190X-10781

At Home Workshops

Swing Trading Essentials *with Jon Markman*

Master the latest techniques and newest methods for reaping even bigger profits by swing trading, direct from the best-selling author of *Swing Trading* and CNBC/MSN Money columnist. Swing trading—or buying stocks for holding periods of a week to 6 months—is fast becoming the new trading paradigm. Now, this well-known expert will guide you through his personal and proven secrets for swing-trading success—in the comfort of your own home.

$99.00.   Item #T190X-1674511 (VHS)
$99.00.   Item #T190X-1674562 (DVD)

Swing Trading *with Oliver Velez*

Finally a video workshop on swing trading! Comes with online manual featuring everything you need to master swing trading and take it to new levels of success. See why one trader says he bought the tape . . . made $700 on a short sale, right off the bat, using the technique. Seriously . . . a quality video.

$99.00.   Item #T190X-11356 (VHS only)

▲ ▲ ▲ ▲ ▲ ▲

These videos along with hundreds of others are available at a discount from Traders' Library. To place an order or to find out more, **call 1-800-272-2855** *or visit our web site at*

www.traderslibrary.com

Intra-Day Trading Tactics *with Greg Capra*

Successful Intra-day trading is a fine art—and Greg Capra is a master of the game. Now, he shares his personal secrets for prospering in this high-intensity arena. Displaying confidence, discipline and patience—the 3 traits of winning traders—he demonstrates how to pool an array of indicators to create a profitable trading protocol that can be used again & again.

$99.00. Item #T190X-41617 (VHS only)

Intra-Day Trading Strategies
Proven Steps to Trading Profits with Jeff Cooper

The famous *Hit & Run Trading* author and TheStreet.com columnist unveils personal weapons for winning in short-term markets. Jeff goes beyond anything he's written, sharing his coveted intra-day strategies with you, one-on-one.

$129.00. Item #T190X-1674508 (VHS)
$129.00. Item #T190X-1674510 (DVD)

The Jack Schwager Trading Course
Your Complete Guide to Mastering the Markets

This comprehensive home study course, from "Market Wizard" Jack Schwager is the ultimate trading workshop. This 12-tape course is incredibly comprehensive. It's easy to follow, understand and apply. It comes with a thick reference manual that reinforces each critical point, and a complete Online Chart companion that allows you to print out and study each chart as you go.

$799.00. Item #T190X-1198400 (VHS)

Call **1-800-272-2855** *or visit our web site at*

www.traderslibrary.com

FREE 2-Week Trial to SwingTracker

Try the best stock charts and market analysis — FREE — for 2 weeks. You'll discover:

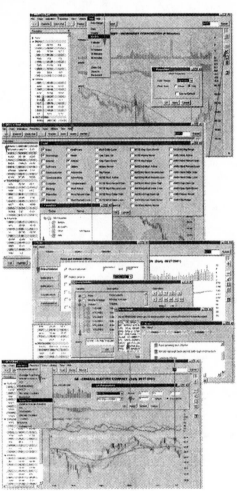

- **SwingTracker v4.0** — a quote, scan and charting software designed specifically for swing & day traders

- **Real-time Intra-day technical charts**

- **Sophisticated stock tools & dozens of technical indicators**

- **Plus many special features** — all right at your fingertips — and all exclusively for swing traders

MrSWING Lite Newsletter .... *FREE*
A Free weekly Newsletter full of swing-trading opportunities. Subscribe and receive a weekly newsletter free of charge, which includes trading master plan opportunities, examples, tools, books, brokers, and more.

Chart of the Week .... *FREE*
Chart of the Week is a free email newsletter devoted to providing insightful charts on a variety of technical topics, delivered directly to your inbox when updated!

SwingLab .... *FREE*
The free Think-Tank for swing-trading patterns coding! Our attempt is to write about and discuss swing queries that produce daily swing trading opportunities in **SwingTracker**.

SwingTracker *RISK-FREE 2-WEEK TRIAL* **$39.95/m**
Find the proven powers in swing trading with SwingTracker v4.0! SwingTracker 4.0 is real-time stock quotes, scan, and charts software, featuring EquiVolume & Force Index. Sign up for a free two-week trial period today.

Best Swing Trading **$249/m**
Posted nightly in our members-only section of the web site. The swing-trading newsletter is perfect for those who want consistent returns, but do not want to sit in front of the computer all day.

OptionSwings Weekly Newsletter **$99.90/m**
Earn 50%-140% per month trading options regardless of market movement. Now with AUTOTRADE!

Sector-Swings Weekly Newsletter. **$59.95/m**
How to trade sectors like a pro! Now with AUTOTRADE!

QQQ-Swings IntraDay Newsletter **$69.95/m**
QQQ-Swings Intra-Day Stock & Options Swing-Trading Alert! Now with AUTOTRADE!

Sector-Swings IntraDay Newsletter **$59.95/m**
Sector-Swings Intra-Day Stock & Options Swing-Trading Alert! Now with AUTOTRADE!

MasterSwings Daily Newsletter **$39.95/m**
MrSwing's Daily Stock Swing-Trading Alerts! You can now receive in-depth swing trading from Larry Swing, every day!

Free 2-Week Trial Offer for U.S. Residents From Investor's Business Daily:

I NVESTOR'S BUSINESS DAILY will provide you with the facts, figures, and objective news analysis you need to succeed.

Investor's Business Daily is formatted for a quick and concise read, to help you make informed and profitable decisions.

To take advantage of this free 2-week trial offer, e-mail us at customerservice@traderslibrary.com or visit our web site at www.traderslibrary.com where you find other free offers as well.

Or call now:

1-800-272-2855 ext T190

Notes

Notes:

About the Author

LARRY D. SPEARS is an editorial consultant based in Amarillo, Texas. A former editor with *The San Jose Mercury* and *The Los Angeles Times*, Mr. Spears now specializes in the production of financial and investment reports.

An active investor and an options trader since 1978, he is the author of several books such as *Commodity Options: Spectacular Profits With Limited Risk*, and *7 Steps to Success Trading Options Online*.

He is also the co-creator and editor of Hume Group Inc.'s Super-Investor Files series; co-author of *Money Magazine's* "100 Steps to Wealth" series; and editor of several stock market advisory letters, as well as other investment publications and articles.